POETRY
APPRECIATION
FOR A-LEVEL

JOHN CARDEN

Hodder & Stoughton

A MEMBER OF THE HODDER HEADLINE GROUP

Orders: please contact Bookpoint Ltd, 39 Milton Park, Abingdon, Oxon
OX14 4TD. Telephone: (44) 01235 400414, Fax: (44) 01235 400454.
Lines are open from 9.00 – 6.00, Monday to Saturday, with a 24 hour
message answering service. Email address: orders@bookpoint.co.uk

British Library Cataloguing in Publication Data
A catalogue record for this title is available from The British Library

ISBN 0 7131 7609 1

First published 1986
Impression number 19 18 17 16 15 14 13 12
Year   2004 2003 2002 2001 2000 1999

Copyright © 1984 Federal Publications (S) Pte Ltd
A member of the Times Publishing Group

Printed in Singapore for Hodder & Stoughton Educational, a division of
Hodder Headline Plc, 338 Euston Road, London NW1 3BH by Mentor
Printers Pte Ltd.

PREFACE

This book is concerned mainly with the nature of poetry and the fundamental issues of how it should be *approached* and *appreciated*. Given the personalised intimacy of poetry — intimacy between the poet and his experience, the poet and the poem, the poet and the reader (and, for that matter, the reader and *his* experience) — such a book must tread warily and, hopefully, sensitively.

Basically the book has two aims. The first is to stimulate and encourage the freedom of personal response in the reader that the intimacy of poetry promotes — indeed, requires, if the communication is to take place at a meaningful level. The second aim is to develop an awareness and understanding of the elements of poetry (form, imagery, rhythm etc.) in order to enrich the quality of that personal response. The basic premise is that, although any given poem may 'say' different things to different people, agreement can be reached as to how the poem seeks to gain its effect. This is what is meant by *appreciation* — as opposed to *criticism* or *judgement*. In this way, a poem not immediately suited to one's personal tastes or preference may still be 'appreciated', even admired.

The book also attempts to cater to a specific need. It seems to me that there is a considerable gap between general books on poetry that attempt to nourish a perceptive interest in poetry in secondary school students and the advanced, specialised observations of, say, an I.A. Richards. The Advanced Level student of English Literature, who is hopefully maturing towards an awareness of the complex and subtle potential of literature, has precious little material to guide him at his own level. Such a person, it is hoped, will benefit most from this book, although the general reader and more advanced specialist should also find things of interest in the following pages.

J.C.
1984

C O N T E N T S

CHAPTER 1

INTRODUCTION

POETRY AND THE STUDENT

This book is designed specifically for students of English Literature at the Advanced Level. It will attempt to give such students a thorough grounding in the basics of poetry analysis and will assume little previous background training or reading on the part of the student in poetry appreciation.

Much emphasis will be placed on *how* the student *approaches* poetry. We cannot all be equally sensitive to the often subtle and delicate vibrations of poetry — any more than we can all run at the same speed or jump the same heights. However, if the approach is correct, any student on an Advanced English course has the potential to understand and enjoy poetry. This goes far beyond any examination success; it can be a gift for life. Students and teachers alike should bear in mind Dr. Johnson's pronouncement that poetry only achieves its intended effect or impact if it delights the reader in some way.

A fundamental problem lies in the difficulty of subjecting something as potentially personal, emotional and evanescent as poetry to the discipline of academic study. Some say the 'spirit' of poetry cannot be 'pinned down' under the microscope of analysis and will quote Wordsworth's famous lines:

> our meddling intellect
>> Mis-shapes the form of things;
>> We murder to dissect.

Yet such a complaint is clearly not valid. When approached in the proper manner, poetry analysis is an enriching and creative process. It is only by looking at a poem in detail that we do justice to the considerable creative effort that went into its crafting. There is also the problem of the teacher's sense of responsibility towards the students and the students' own expectations — both haunted by the spectre of passing examinations. (It is worth remembering that we are, as teachers, forced to keep examinations in mind — no matter how desirable it may be not to do so; we can be sure the students will.) Because of this, there is a temptation — on both sides — to cling to "correct" readings, stock responses, seemingly quantifiable mechanics of poetry (such as *form* and *metre*) etc. Because of this, the *essential* aspect of *personal response* by the student to poetry is lost. The mechanics of poetry — those aspects that may be learnt 'formula-fashion' — take over the whole process; and the whole process quickly becomes deadeningly "mechanical". Instead of a journey towards some sort of discovery (about the writer, or the poem, or life, or oneself) which poetry should represent, the landmarks (i.e., the mechanics) become destinations in their own right and the more significant regions beyond or beneath the poem remain undiscovered.

The first crucial element, then, comes from within ourselves, from the spirit in which we approach the poem. This should hold true for all aspects of the study of literature, yet the student will still feel safer with 'set texts', believing he can 'get by' through assimilating details about themes, characterization, style, background etc. With the unseen Practical Criticism papers there are no such straws of comfort. If the student has not consciously developed the ability to respond to poetry, the final result will always be shallow and unconvincing.

POETRY AND THE NON-NATIVE STUDENT

There is an ever-increasing number of students studying English poetry, particularly in Africa and Asia, who are non-native speakers of English. Such students face specific problems. For although it is readily accepted that good literature will always transcend the confines of time and space, there remain special considerations for such students.

Such problems do not relate to deficiencies in background information, whether social or historical, as these are easily supplied and overcome. Nor do they relate to cultural or geographical differences. I have known a poem like 'To Autumn' by John Keats enjoyed and appreciated as much by students in Singapore as by students in the inner-city slum areas of Liverpool — and neither group of students had first-hand experience of the particular rural beauty celebrated in that poem.

The basic problem for non-native students lies in the language of poetry. By language here I do not mean difficult grammatical constructions or unfamiliar vocabulary. It lies more in what I.A. Richards termed the 'sensuous apprehension' of language that is often so crucial to poetry. In other words, certain subtleties or nuances of a line, or a phrase, or a single word, are often used by poets to bring strength, or delicacy, or surprise to their verse. The poet may 'play' such words against their expected, or normal, or current associations. Or he may use a word in its pure sense, or for its old-fashioned associations. He may also use a word with different, yet equally viable, shadings of meaning. Take, for instance, the lines from William Blake's 'London':

> In every cry of every Man,
> In every Infant's cry of fear,
> In every voice, in every ban,
> The mind-forg'd manacles I hear.

The word "ban" here has several possible meanings — political or legal prohibition, a curse, public condemnation, marriage banns proclaiming the intention to marry — and, in the context of this poem criticizing social conditions in London at the time, all these associations, or shadings, are relevant. An even more extreme example is the sonnet by Shakespeare that persistently employs the word "will", fluctuating between at least six possible meanings of the word — including a *pun* on the abbreviated form of the poet's own first name!

Not being constantly immersed in the type of 'native' English in which English poets inevitably write, the non-native student may well have difficulty with these subtleties of language. Because poetry makes such frequent use of such subtleties, this is an important consideration. There is a similar problem with speech rhythms — where pronunciation and stress patterns may differ in the native and non-native speakers. The flow and movement of the verse will only be grasped if the poem is read in the stress and intonation patterns in which they were written.

There is no easy way around these difficulties. Quite simply, the non-native student must make every effort to acquaint himself with the *reading* of English poetry as far as possible, both in terms of listening to experienced readers and practising, aloud, with others and by himself.

PRESENT FORMAT

This book is in four sections. The first short, yet crucial, section deals with the way in which the student should *approach* poetry. The second section looks at the *elements* of poetry — subject and theme, tone, rhythm, imagery, rhyme, intention — in terms of their characteristics, function and potential, both in general and as they relate specifically to five 'reference' poems. The section on elements also includes relevant, short exercises where appropriate. The third section offers guidance on how the student should approach, arrange and present a written poetry appreciation analysis and includes two complete sample analyses to illustrate poetry appreciation 'in action'. The fourth section provides a series of poems for full-length analysis, including several examples from past Advanced Level English papers.

At the end of the book, there is a *glossary* containing all the terms of a technical nature with which the student should be familiar and capable of using appropriately in his own written analysis.

CHAPTER 2

APPROACH

GENERAL CONSIDERATIONS

It is a pity that most students continue to regard confronting a new poem for the first time as a daunting, intimidating task throughout their entire course. In an academic sense, it is inevitable that we feel apprehensive or inadequate as we approach a new area of study, yet the feeling is even more marked when it comes to unseen poetry appreciation. There is, however, an obvious irony here. Of all the texts a student will come across in the various fields of his academic studies, literature is the one area where the text in question was neither written by, nor for, academics. Indeed, the primary function of literature has little to do with academic processes — unless we take the word "educational" in its wider sense of "learning about life". Such a statement may well be obvious, but the implications behind it, which are so crucial to how we approach literature in the first place, are not always acknowledged. In other words, the student need not — in fact, must not — see poetry appreciation in the standard academic manner of knowledge extension or problem solving. The piece of work before him may not necessarily be there to develop what has gone before, or to tie in with the previous lesson. Nor is it intended, again in the academic sense, to test him or catch him out. Unlike other subjects, it does not involve the passing on of knowledge or facts from the informed expert to the uninformed student. What he will find is an offering — creative, well wrought, deeply considered, personalized observations that will call on the student's own experience of life and ask him to relate it to that of others.

The student, then, must forget the standard procedures of instruction and information-giving when it comes to poetry appreciation — no easy task, as it will probably be all he has known to date. This is something many students, used to being 'spoon-fed' with all they will require, find difficult to accept. The student must be prepared to relate *positively* to the poem before him. A poem simply cannot be 'taught' — though some teachers are unfortunately unaware of this. Guidance, certainly, is needed, but the student must see his role as an active one. He cannot be given a response; it must be his own. In the final analysis, poetry is all about *responding*. Attempts at second-hand responses are painfully obvious in the work of students who, for whatever reason, have failed to make the effort.

In spite of all this, many teachers fail to structure their approach to poetry courses in the light of such implications. Poetry will deal with sensitive, personal, even intimate issues, so the teacher also has to keep the students' position constantly in mind. Apart from coming into contact with such material for, perhaps, the first time, the group will probably comprise of diffident young people, facing a new type of academic discipline, perhaps in a new environment, probably in the company of strangers (perhaps even the opposite sex) for the first time. Because the discussion method — open exchange and drawing out, between student and teacher, and student and student — is central to any successful poetry course, we can see just how delicate the situation is. Yet it is a far from impossible situation and such sessions can become the most rewarding a student will experience at this stage of his academic career, as they help bridge the gap between the one-sided, passive, soaking up of knowledge of one's early education and the more active, research type of growing awareness of one's more mature studies.

THE STUDENT AND PERSONAL RESPONSE

The student must clear his mind of certain presuppositions about his poetry course before he starts. Firstly, he will be working in a discipline where, by and large, there are no right or wrong answers. There is no one correct reading of any given poem — a state of apparent vagueness that frequently horrifies many students. There is, of course, what may be termed a 'received opinion' of the poem in question — an opinion, reached, perhaps, after years of critical attention, as to what the poem is about, or means. Even this may be fruitfully (rather than wilfully or perversely) challenged from time to time. The student may come to cling to this strategy of 'received opinions' about poems, but he must realize that in the end, in the examination room, it will be his ability to respond perceptively and critically to poetry that will be under the microscope. He will not have the benefit of the opinions of others. Quite simply, it will be a question of how the student has approached his course — whether he has positively made the effort to develop his awareness, his critical faculty for discriminating reading and, significantly, his confidence for making detailed, relevant observations about poetry; whether, in fact, he has shown himself capable of 'opening' himself to literature and actively responding to it.

Secondly, having accepted that some form of response is essential, it is necessary to clarify the type of response. Here there is a danger inherent in the terminology we use. Rather than seeing such courses as **Practical Criticism**, I feel we should think more in terms of **Poetry Appreciation**. The distinction is not as petty as it may appear. Many students tend to take the term "criticism" too literally — in the pejorative sense of criticize — and adopt the role of the reviewer or even, worse still, judge and jury. This quickly becomes related to another damaging preconception — the notion of 'good' and 'bad' poetry. This becomes particularly negative when the students, confronted with two poems for comparison, feel the examiner is testing their ability to select and praise the good poem and spend most of their time trying to assess which of the two poems this one is. Of course some poems are more effective than others and of course the student's own preference is welcomed. However, a student's attempt to "vote" for the good poem, which dismisses or praises a poem on a superficial or over-subjective basis and directs the analysis in support of this view-point, will not constitute true poetry appreciation or analysis. It would be more productive for the student to assume that there is some merit to be found in whatever poem he is given — if there is not then the examiners have been wasting everybody's time — and to try and appreciate what that might be. Another problem here is that people tend to associate the word "appreciate" with "liking", or having a preference for. Such an association is possible, yet not essential. A diamond expert, for instance, will be able to expound on and outline the merits of a particular diamond — its cut, or its clarity etc — even though the piece may not be to his own taste or liking. He can still appreciate its qualities — qualities that may make it attractive to others. The student's attitude should be similar. The poem he is offered may not be to his taste, or deeply meaningful or moving to him, yet the question he must ask himself is what is there in it, in its own right as a poem, that may be deemed of value.

APPROACHING THE POEM

So far we have dealt with the question of approach in general. There remains now the way in which the student actually confronts a specific poem. The most crucial aspect here, is that the student must be prepared to 'live' with the poem for a while. He must avoid the temptation of rushing into hasty observations or ill-considered judgements. This is especially difficult to do in the time-pressure situation of the examination room. Yet all serious literature is demanding, and poetry, with its deliberate, often intense, concentration of detail and effect, especially so.

Nobody can hope to make important or profound observations, on a poem they have never seen before, on the basis of a couple of quick readings. Students often deplore their own dullness when they still cannot make much sense of a poem after several readings. The simple fact is that until you have begun to feel your way into a poem and begin to sense an awareness of what it is about, it is pointless to say anything. In the class/tutorial/discussion setting, the comments of others may lead the student 'into' the poem, help him begin to focus on its details and issues. In the examination situation, only further reading can possibly help. The important (and difficult) thing here is to avoid freezing before the poem — of going blank in a sort of numb panic. The student must try and stay 'open' to the poem, to continue working at it in a positive way — as I say, to 'live' with it for a while. An ideal pattern would probably involve two straightforward readings of the poem, followed by several further readings that would involve the making of notes, marking of lines, underlining of words etc. — a process probably lasting about twenty minutes. It would still make more sense to spend even longer on reading if necessary and finally have something meaningful to say, rather than rushing into cursory comments after a few confused struggles with the poem. Remember, it is the quality of the reading that will dictate the quality of the written analysis.

There is one final, important consideration about the time factor in examinations which students often forget — and this holds good for all subjects. Examinations are not a race. What is being examined is not the student's ability to think and write at speed. It is the quality of what he has to say. The time allocated for an answer will not be unreasonable and will always allow the student adequate time to answer the question as fully as required.

Another important aspect of reading poetry that the student must remember is that nearly all poetry is meant to be read aloud. This is not a problem in class, but the student will have to consciously develop the ability to hear a poem in his mind. It is here that the non-native speaker of the language must make extra efforts if he is to prevent himself from being disadvantaged. Such a student's speech pattern of pronunciation, stress and intonation may be different from those the poet has used. As I have already said, such a student will have to try and acquaint himself as fully as possible with the reading of English poetry — both by listening to others and by practising himself. If he does not hear the poem as the poet intended, he may miss much of the movement and music (and possibly meaning) of the verse.

In the course of his prolonged reading of a new poem, the student will also need the confidence to overcome one of the major difficulties that arise with unseen poetry. This relates partly to what was said before about "freezing". Students frequently quail (and often surrender) before what strike them as obscure, impenetrable ideas, vague or veiled allusions or references, difficult vocabulary or grammatical structures — and this applies equally to native and non-native speakers. A psychological block or barrier to the poem that has caused such discomfort is quickly, sometimes irredeemably, erected. Once again, the only possible remedy is patient and, as far as possible, calm reading. The poem is not a code or puzzle to be deciphered. Rather than bemoaning inwardly a cleverness (or perverseness) to which he is not party, the student should concentrate on asking himself why has the poet chosen such a mode of expression. Such a question will lead inevitably into the heart of the poem as the way in which it is written will always relate directly to what it has to say. Wordsworth once described the poet as a 'man speaking to men'. This should be a guiding maxim for all students of poetry appreciation for the confidence and direction it will bring to their approach.

RESPONSE AND RELEVANCE

If the student can bring such an approach to his reading of poetry, he will avoid one other perennial pitfall. A close, attentive reading of the actual poem in front of him will keep the student's analysis relevant to that poem. In this way, it will avoid falling back on conventional responses — where the student makes a quick assessment of the subject-matter (e.g. the death of a child, the beauty of a winter landscape etc.) and then unfolds a series of conventional ideas about such a theme. Such generalized analyses move away from what the specific poem given actually has to say. It is worth remembering that some of the most memorable poetry derives its strength from handling 'conventional' themes and ideas in an unconventional or unexpected manner.

EXERCISES

1. Read the following poem, by Thomas Hardy, several times to yourself, then at least once out aloud.

THE VOICE

Woman much missed, how you call to me, call to me,
Saying that now you are not as you were
When you had changed from the one who was all to me,
But as at first, when our day was fair.

Can it be you that I hear? Let me view you, then,   5
Standing as when I drew near to the town
Where you would wait for me: yes, as I knew you, then,
Even to the original air-blue gown!

Or is it only the breeze, in its listlessness
Travelling across the wet mead to me here,   10

You being ever dissolved to wan wistlessness,
Heard no more again far or near?

Thus I; faltering forward,
Leaves around me falling,
Wind oozing thin through the thorn from norward,   15
And the woman calling.

a. What do you imagine is the situation behind this poem that prompted the poet to write it?

b. What do you understand by lines 11-12?

c. How does the poet feel in his present situation? Which parts of the poem best convey these feelings?

d. Why do you think the poet alters the structure of the poem in the final stanza?

e. Do you find the poem 'moving'? What are your feeling towards, (i) the poet, (ii) the poem?

f. Why do you feel the poet has written such a poem?

2. The following poem by Wilfred Owen describes a young, dying soldier being removed from the front line of battle during World War I. Again, give the poem several close, attentive readings, out loud if possible.

Move him into the sun —
Gently its touch awoke him once,
At home, whispering of fields unsown.
Always it woke him, even in France,
Until this morning and this snow.   5
If anything might rouse him now
The kind old sun will know.

Think how it wakes the seeds —
Woke, once, the clays of a cold star.
Are limbs, so dear-achieved, are sides,   10
Full-nerved — still warm — too hard to stir?
Was it for this the clay grew tall?
— O what made fatuous sunbeams toil
To break earth's sleep at all?

a. What do you understand the poem's final three lines to mean?

b. How would you describe the poet's handling of his theme?

c. Why do you think the poet makes such constant use of the sun?

d. The poet talks little about the actual dying soldier. What do you think is his main concern in this poem?

e. Much has been written about the waste of human life in times of war. How effective do you find this poem as a statement of this issue? Is poetry a proper medium for dealing with such matters?

f. Do you feel that there are certain areas of the human experience that are so intense and personal (love, war, death etc.) that they cannot be adequately expressed in words — no matter how hard writers and poets try?

CHAPTER 3

E L E M E N T S   O F   A N A L Y S I S

Poetry may be seen in terms of various elements such as form, imagery, rhythm, rhyme etc. In fact, it is more convenient and productive for us to view a poem on this divisional basis, both in written analysis and discussion. There is often the criticism that by dissecting a poem in this way we are somehow going against the true spirit of poetry. Yet the poet will have toiled long to craft these diverse elements in just the right way and it is only by analysing these details in depth that we can fully appreciate the poem and do justice to the creative effort that went into its making. What we must bear constantly in mind, however, is that these diverse elements of the poem are all working together, towards an integrated whole. Each aspect represents only part of the overall design and it is this design — i.e. why the poem was written in the first place and what the poet is trying to achieve or communicate — that must remain our prime concern. In other words, we must not become so obsessed with a poem's use of imagery, or rhyme, that we come to see them as ends in their own right. They are not. They are used for a specific purpose, as part of the design.

Students sometimes acquire a mass of information about those aspects of poetry they feel most comfortable with and then concentrate almost exclusively on those aspects, often trotting out a wealth of frequently irrelevant background information on say, form and imagery, while ignoring other aspects, perhaps rhythm and rhyme, which they do n.t feel so sure about. If such students confront a poem by Hopkins or Dylan Thomas (two poets who made extensive explorations into the potential of rhythm and rhyme) they will miss much of what the poem is trying to achieve.

The student must seek to acquire as full an awareness as possible of all the elements of poetry to be in a position to concentrate relevantly on the particular elements that are highlighted in any given poem. Because of the degree of integration and harmony present in most poetry, it is some-what arbitrary to isolate these elements too rigidly. However, for the purpose of this book and in order to offer the student some insight into the nature and function of these elements, we will take them separately, one by one.

Although we will look at the characteristics of such elements in general, it will be useful to relate them to specific instances as we proceed. For this purpose, I have selected five poems as "reference poems". These poems represent a variety of theme and type as well as being poetry written in different ages. The student will receive most help from this method if he acquaints himself with the poems initially and then refers to them again as they are analysed in their various elements.

Reference Poems

Poem A

MUTABILITY

We are as clouds that veil the midnight moon;
    How restlessly they speed, and gleam, and quiver,
Streaking the darkness radiantly! — yet soon
    Night closes round, and they are lost forever:

Or like forgotten lyres, whose dissonant strings   5
    Give various response to each varying blast,
To whose frail frame no second motion brings
    One mood or modulation like the last.

We rest. — A dream has power to poison sleep;
    We rise. — One wandering thought pollutes the day;   10
We feel, conceive or reason, laugh or weep;
    Embrace fond woe, or cast our cares away:

It is the same! — For,be it joy or sorrow,
    The path of its departure still is free:
Man's yesterday may ne'er be like his morrow;   15
    Nought may endure but Mutability.

Poem B

MUSÉE DES BEAUX ARTS[1]

About suffering they were never wrong,
The Old Masters[2]: how well they understood
Its human position; how it takes place
While someone else is eating or opening a window or just walking
    dully along;
How, when the aged are reverently, passionately waiting   5
For the miraculous birth, there always must be
Children who did not specially want it to happen, skating
On a pond at the edge of the wood:
They never forgot
That even the dreadful martyrdom must run its course   10
Anyhow in a corner, some untidy spot
Where the dogs go on with their doggy life and the
    torturer's horse
Scratches its innocent behind on a tree.

In Brueghel's 'Icarus'[3], for instance: how everything turns away
Quite leisurely from the disaster; the plowman may   15
Have heard the splash, the forsaken cry,
But for him it was not an important failure; the sun shone
As it had to on the white legs disappearing into the green
Water; and the expensive delicate ship that must have seen
Something amazing, a boy falling out of the sky,   20
Had somewhere to get to and sailed calmly on.

[1]*Museum of Fine Arts*, in Belgium, whose art gallery contains the painting in question.

[2]A group of painters, specifically of the Flemish school of the fifteenth and sixteenth centuries.

[3]The *Icarus* painting of Pieter Brueghel. Icarus ventured to fly on artificial wings made of wax. Because of his over-ambition, he flew too near the sun, causing his fatal fall as the wings melted. In this painting the legs disappear in a corner of the painting, with the rest of the composition — notably a plowman and finely-rigged ship — appearing unaware of the disaster.

Poem C

THE DEVIL'S ADVICE TO STORY-TELLERS

Lest men suspect your tale to be untrue,
Keep probability — some say — in view.
But my advice to story-tellers is:
Weigh out no gross of probabilities,
Nor yet make diligent transcriptions of   5
Known instances of virtue, crime or love.
To forge a picture that will pass for true,
Do conscientiously what liars do —
Born liars, not the lesser sort that raid
The mouths of others for their stock-in-trade: 10
Assemble, first, all casual bits and scraps
That may shake down into a world perhaps;
People this world, by chance created so,
With random persons whom you do not know —
The teashop sort, or travelers in a train   15
Seen once, guessed idly at, not seen again;
Let the erratic course they steer surprise
Their own and your own and your readers' eyes;
Sigh then, or frown, but leave (as in despair)
Motive and end and moral in the air;   20
Nice contradiction between fact and fact
Will make the whole read human and exact.

Poem D

SHAKESPEARE

Others abide our question. Thou art free.
We ask and ask — Thou smilest and art still,
Out-topping knowledge. For the loftiest hill,
Who to the stars uncrowns his majesty,

Planting his steadfast footsteps in the sea,   5
Making the heaven of heavens his dwelling place,
Spares but the cloudy border of his base
To the foiled searching of mortality;
And thou, who didst the stars and sunbeams know,
Self-schooled, self-scanned, self-honoured, self-secure,   10
Didst tread on earth unguessed at. — Better so!

All pains the immortal spirit must endure,
All weakness which impairs, all griefs which bow,
Find their sole speech in that victorious brow.

Poem E

TO AUTUMN

Season of mists and mellow fruitfulness
    Close bosom-friend of the maturing sun;
Conspiring with him how to load and bless
    With fruit the vines that round the thatch-eaves run;
To bend with apples the mossed cottage-trees,   5
    And fill all fruit with ripeness to the core;
        To swell the gourd and plump the hazel shells
    With a sweet kernel; to set budding more,
And still more, later flowers for the bees,
Until they think warm days will never cease,   10
        For Summer has oe'rbrimmed their clammy cells.

Who hath not seen thee oft amid thy store?
    Sometimes whoever seeks abroad may find
Thee sitting careless on a granary floor,
    Thy hair soft-lifted by the winnowing wind;   15
Or on a half-reaped furrow sound asleep,
    Drowsed with the fume of poppies, while thy hook[1]
        Spares the next swath and all its twinéd flowers:
And sometimes like a gleaner thou dost keep
    Steady thy laden head across a brook;   20
    Or by a cider-press, with patient look,
        Thou watchest the last oozings hours by hours.

Where are the songs of Spring? Aye, where are they?
    Think not of them, thou hast thy music too —
While barred clouds bloom the soft-dying day,   25
    And touch the stubble-pains with rosy hue;
Then in a wailful choir the small gnats mourn
    Among the river sallows[2], borne aloft
        Or sinking as the light wind lives or dies;
And full-grown lambs loud bleat from hilly bourn[3];
    Hedge-crickets sing; and now with treble soft
    The redbreast whistles from a garden croft[4];
        And gathering swallows twitter in the skies.

[1] scythe

[2] willows

[3] region

[4] enclosed plot of farmland

CHAPTER 4

S U B J E C T

The first step towards understanding a poem lies in making general observations as to what the poem is about; that is, its theme or subject-matter. At a mechanical level, this can involve actually paraphrasing the poem or summarizing its content. Most students feel that comprehending the poem, or actually making some sense of it, constitutes the main difficulty of poetry appreciation. Yet students often neglect to take this obvious first step and prefer to hurry into more profound — and mark-scoring — insights and observations. After the initial readings, we will not yet be concerned with the poem's overall intention or deeper purpose. The opening comments will only relate to meaning in a surface sense (what the poet is talking about, his *topic*), rather than in the wider sense of what the poem is basically trying to communicate as a whole. Such opening remarks should not be too elaborate. They are there to provide a framework, a direction for the analysis of the other elements and the overall intention of the poem that will follow.

SUBJECT AND THE REFERENCE POEMS

Poem A   This poem is deliberately chosen because it contains one of the typical 'stumbling-blocks' outlined earlier — i.e. the prominence of a word or concept that may be unfamiliar to the student. Ideally we would like to imagine that most students undertaking an Advanced Level English course would be familiar with a word like *mutable* but, from experience, we know that this would not be the case. However, if the student approaches the poem in the way that has been suggested, he should be able to comprehend what the poet is trying to say. A statement of this poem's subject-matter should be something along the lines of: "In this poem the poet is considering the impermanent nature of our existence, where nothing lasts forever in its original state, no matter how beautiful or intense it may be".

Poem B   Similarly, this poem contains possibly unfamiliar allusions. In this case, such references would be accompanied by explanatory notes, such as I have included here. Again they do not hinder any meaningful grasp of the poem. Here our statement on subject might run: "The poet is concerned with how little one individual's moment of crisis or suffering seems to affect the daily routine of the rest of us. Using Brueghel's painting of the Icarus legend as a focal point, the poem illustrates how ordinary life continues, unaffected by such an amazing catastrophe".

Poem C   The theme of this poem is a literary one. Our opening statement would be something like: "The poet here is concerned with removing certain misconceptions about story-telling and offers the would-be story-teller his own views as to what constitutes true fiction".

Poem D   This also has a literary subject, which can be summarized as: "This poem is addressed to, and in praise of, Shakespeare. The poet comments on the nature of Shakespeare's achievement and the value it holds for the rest of us".

Poem E   The theme of this poem is a perennial one in poetry and can be stated as: "This poem celebrates the beauty of Nature as it appears during the season of autumn, paying sensuous tribute to the rich, ripened fullness of its aspects during this time of the year".

Such observations as the above do not represent particularly profound statements about the given reference poems. However, the process of considering and expressing a poem's subject-matter will help to focus the student's attention on the deeper implications that lie within the poem.

CHAPTER 5

F O R M

IMPORTANCE OF FORM

Many students fail to see the importance of *form* in poetry. They feel it is something chosen almost at random — "Now let me see, I haven't written a sonnet for a week or two, perhaps I had better do one next" — and then forgotten, left to take care of itself. Two basic points must be realized about form. Firstly, a serious poet thinks as long about the form of his poem, the one that will most suit and best convey what he has to say, as he does about the other elements of his craft. Ultimately there will be a significant reason for the poet choosing the form he settles on — a reason which will have a direct bearing on what the poem is actually trying to achieve. Students sometimes content themselves with spotting the form, naming it, then feeling that is sufficient to score the necessary 'plus' for form. Yet the student must not only ask "what form is this poem in?", he must also develop this into "why was such a form chosen?" Actually, this is a golden rule of all poetry appreciation; 'why?' is always a far more important question that 'what?' Instead of contenting himself with such comments as, say, "alliteration is used in line three", the student should be more concerned with assessing what such an instance of alliteration is contributing to the poem at that point. The technical terms of poetry appreciation are important. Such concepts as alliteration, metaphor, onomatopoeia etc. must be assimilated and then used. Yet they are not an end in their own right. They are reference points that provide the student with a specialized and specific 'language' in which to develop his analysis of the *effect* that such devices produce in the examples before him.

The second point about form is that, in spite of the seemingly fixed nature that will appear to govern the writing of a sonnet, or blank verse, form must not be seen as a concrete, inflexible set of rules and structures. No matter how rigid the form may appear, an imaginative poet will always seek to develop, expand and re-examine all areas of poetic potential — and form is also open to such exploration and experimentation. Again, one must focus on the poem that is presented. Certainly background information is crucial, but we may have to adapt or modify such knowledge in the light of a given example. It must not harden into inflexible, short-sighted, preconceived notions.

DIFFERENT FORMS OF ENGLISH POETRY

Blank Verse

Over the centuries, more English poetry has been written in blank verse than in any other form. Although it is used far less in modern times (which, in literary terms means, by and large, anything written after 1918 where there has been a marked movement away from rigidly structured forms of poetry) it has remained a form that attracts many poets (notably in the work of T.S. Eliot). This is probably because many of the finest achievements of English poetry (Shakespeare's plays, Milton's *Paradise Lost*, Wordsworth's *Prelude*, Browning's monologues — to name but a few) have been written in this form.

Blank verse is described as *unrhymed iambic pentameter*. This rather frightening mouthful indicates three characteristics. Firstly, and obviously, it is unrhymed in the sense that it is a form of poetry that does not make use of rhyme. The second and third characteristics relate to what is called *metre*. A more detailed examination of the concept of metre will be found in the section, *RHYTHM*, as it bears a more direct relationship to that element of poetry. Simply put for our present purpose, metre in poetry corresponds to the fixed time patterns (e.g. waltz time, 4/4 time) of musical beats in a bar, for the more structured and traditional forms of poetry. Following guidelines from classical literature, it was felt that poetry should be so thoroughly formal that there should be fixed rules about number of syllables per line and the pattern of stressed and unstressed syllables within that line. For all practical purposes, the student today need not concern himself with the somewhat artificial concept of metre, although it does have certain broad implications (again see *RHYTHM*). Pentameter basically means that each line of the verse will have ten syllables. In its intricate technicalities, it further means that these ten syllables can be divided into five units of two syllables each. Within these units, known as *feet*, there is a fixed pattern of metre — i.e. an unstressed syllable, followed by a stressed syllable, as in "cŏncérn", "dĕfeát". (In such notification (˘) means an unstressed syllable, (´) a stressed syllable.) This is the metric pattern known as *iambic*. Although such a pattern exists in blank verse, no poetry is ever read according to its metre — as the section, *RHYTHM* shows. If it were to be read metrically, it would merely produce a dreadful *tee tum, tee tum, tee tum, tee tum* repetition.

In Milton's *Paradise Lost* we find:

> That to the height of this great Argument
> I may assert Eternal Providence,
> And justify the ways of God to men.

The lines do not rhyme. There are ten syllables in each line. Reduced to an iambic pentameter pattern, the lines can appear:

> Thăt tó / tĥe heíght / ŏf thís / grĕat Ár / gŭmént
> Ĭ máy / ašsért / Ĕtér / năl Pŕo / vĭdeńce
> Ańd jús / tĭfý / tĥe wáys / ŏf Gód / tŏ mén.

These, then, are the standard characteristics by which we may recognize blank verse.

It must be repeated that these guidelines are not seen as immutable laws. Blank verse may occasionally use rhyme for a particular effect, either at the end of lines, or within a single line. Shakespeare frequently concludes a scene written in blank verse with a *couplet* — i.e. two lines that rhyme together. A poet will not make his verse so contrived or mechanical that every line will have exactly ten syllables. The celebrated opening of the poem we have just quoted, *Paradise Lost* —

> Of Man's First Disobedience, and the Fruit
> Of that Forbidd'n Tree ...

has eleven syllables. Yet the poet has no intention of losing the solemn, ringing tones of that striking proclamation by searching for substitute words that produce ten syllables in the line.

However, what is more important an issue is why should a poet choose this form? What can it bring to his treatment of his theme that other forms of poetry do not? Again, certain general observations may be made.

Blank verse is a form of poetry that is particularly suited to *longer poetry* for two main reasons. Firstly, it is a structured, even form. As such it will keep a longer poem tightly-knit and help prevent it from becoming loose or rambling. It brings unity and a sense of movement and purpose. Secondly, although it is structured, it is not constrained by the need to rhyme. Freedom from this constraint allows the poet to bring greater variety to the pacing of the poem as a whole. Without rhymed line endings, he is allowed to introduce the occasional use of slightly longer, or shorter lines. Such lines do not jar, or strike us as awkward, without rhyme. It also enables him to run one line, or series of lines, freely into the following line without pause — known as *enjambement* or *run on lines* — or to break lines in the middle, perhaps with dramatic punctuation such as dashes, exclamation and question marks. So the blank verse poet paces his poem — now freely flowing, or slow and solemn, then harsh and disjointed — as it suits the movement of his verse. Blank verse, then, offers these two essential possibilities to the poet: a strong sense of unity and considerable potential for variety.

It is also possible to outline two broad traditions of blank verse: *heroic blank verse* and *dramatic blank verse*. As a literary concept, heroic has little to do with the modern associations of "hero". It refers to writing that is elevated or grand in its style, deliberately (at its worst, self-consciously) formal or high-flown. The subject-matter of heroic writing tends to be the monumental events from religion, history, myth, etc. On the whole, heroic blank verse tends to be more descriptive or narrative, philosophi-cal or contemplative than dramatic blank verse — typified by the grand manner of Milton. In this passage, however, Wordsworth uses a form of heroic blank verse for a tale of simple rustic folk. 'Michael' is the tale of an old shepherd who is devoted to his only son and is left a broken man by the son's dissolute ways and desertion of the family:

> There is a comfort in the strength of love;
> 'Twill make a thing endurable, which else
> Would overset the brain, or break the heart;
> I have conversed with more than one who well
> Remember the Old Man, and what he was
> Years after he had heard this heavy news.

If heroic blank verse makes use of the harmony and strength that the form of blank verse helps produce, then dramatic blank verse makes use of its variety. Here we will feel a strong sense of a scene taking place before us, or a voice speaking directly, or of a tormented mind in conflict with itself. The word dramatic means having the qualities of a drama or play. Dramatic blank verse therefore, tends to be more vivid and immediate and have a greater, more varied sense of movement than heroic blank verse. If Milton stands as the great exponent of the heroic tradition, then Shakespeare is undoubtedly the counterpart for the dramatic. Browning was another poet to develop the dramatic potential of blank verse. In the opening of 'Fra Lippi Lippo', the irascible, eccentric medieval monk and painter, Fra Lippi Lippo, is apprehended late one night by the constables of the watch:

> I am poor brother Lippo, by your leave!
> You need not clap your torches to my face.
> Zooks, what's to blame? you think you see a monk!
> What, tis past midnight, and you go the rounds,
> And here you catch me at an alley's end
> Where sportive ladies leave their doors ajar?
> The Carmine's my cloister: hunt it up,
> Do — harry out, if you must show your zeal,
> Whatever rat, there, haps on his wrong hole,
> And nip each softling of a wee white mouse,
> Weke, weke, that's crept to keep him company!

Because of the rhythmic shifts, — brought about largely by the use of punctuation such as exclamation and question marks, dashes and colons in the middle of lines — and strikingly colloquial language, we can vividly hear and see the scene taking place. This is a basic difference between heroic and dramatic blank verse. In the former we are told about character or thought or situation; in the latter, as with drama itself, we infer such things from what we see and hear actually taking place.

It would be unwise to press such notions of two traditions of blank verse too far, yet they do help to highlight some of the aspects of this form of poetry. Blank verse has been used by a great variety of poets, for differing reasons, and to different effect.

Heroic Couplets

This form is also known as *Rhyming Couplets*. The line length (ten syllables) and metrical pattern are the same as blank verse, but couplets use rhyme, on consecutive lines, in pairs (i.e. line one will rhyme with line two, line three with line four, and so on). It is, therefore, *rhymed iambic pentameter*. With such a rhyme pattern, such poetry tends to move in a steady, undramatic manner in separate, two-line units. In this way a poet can present a series of clearly defined details, or develop an argument in a gradual accumulation that will gather weight and momentum as the poem proceeds. The immediate nearness of the rhyme gives the poem a neat, rounded, complete feeling and a sense that the poet is skilfully in control at all times. Such couplet rhyming tends to be pointed and emphatic and holds considerable potential for humorous, especially satiric, poetry. Its precision and orderliness as a poetic form attracted the poets of the Augustan *Age of Reason* era in English literary history, where it evolved as a medium for sophisticated, urbane and witty satire — its two most impressive practitioners being Dryden and Pope. The frequent savagery of the satirical attacks on leading figures of the time by such poets was delivered in the balanced, controlled, civilized smoothness of heroic couplets — and were all the more effective for it. Take, for instance, Dryden's diatribe against the Earl of Shaftesbury, whom he characterizes as Achitophel, in the poem 'Absalom and Achitophel':

> Great Wits are sure to Madness near alli'd
> And thin partitions do their Bounds divide:
> Else, why should he, with Wealth and Honour blest,
> Refuse his Age the needful Hours of Rest?
> Punish a Body which he could not please;
> Bankrupt of Life, yet Prodigal of Ease?
> And all to leave, what with his toil he won,
> To that unfeather'd, two-legg'd thing, a Son:
> Got while his Soul did huddled Notions try;
> And born a shapeless lump, like Anarchy.

> In friendship false, implacable in Hate:
> Resolved to Ruin or to Rule the State.

The detailed and pointed insults accumulate in the course of such descriptions, each time highlighted with a humorous and telling rhyme. In spite of the venom and contempt behind the attack, the balance and control that comes from the form persuades us that a sophisticated and intelligent mind is at work here. The final couplet is a particularly fine example of the balance and pointed emphasis that can be achieved by a skilful poet with heroic couplets.

This form of poetry, however, is not limited to satire and humour only. Nothing could be further in tone and intention from the passage just quoted from Dryden than Ben Jonson's poem on the death of his first son:

> Rest in soft peace, and, ask'd, say here doth lie
> BEN. JONSON his best piece of poetry.
> For whose sake, hence-forth, all his vows be such,
> As what he loves may never like too much.

Like blank verse, heroic couplets are usually used for longer poems, yet this poem by Jonson, written in heroic couplets, has only twelve lines. Also removed from the type of poetry Pope and Dryden wrote, yet like Jonson, using the heavy, pronounced rhythm of this form to more sombre effect, is Goldsmith's 'Deserted Village'. There is also poetry written in couplets with lines of less than ten syllables (usually eight). This couplet rhyme scheme will still offer the same possibilities as heroic couplets, though such poetry will usually be lighter in touch, less serious in intention and quicker in movement. Swift's 'Verses on the Death of Dr. Swift' is a good example:

> He gave the little Wealth he had,
> To build a House for Fools and Mad:
> And show'd by one satiric touch,
> No nation wanted it so much.

Free Verse

This is the form of poetry that has become predominant in the twentieth-century. It is often confused with blank verse by students but is, in fact, very different. It refers to poetry that does not have lines of regular, or equal length; obsolete ideas about metre are done away with altogether; and there is rarely any rhyme (although there may be on occasion). The twentieth-century has seen rebellions against standard doctrines in all the arts. It has been a period of experimentation that has led to such things as cubism and surrealism in painting, the compositions of Stockhausen and John Cage in music and the *Theatre of the Absurd* in drama. A similar development in poetry led to free verse. Earlier poets had to consider the potential or suitability of the structured forms of poetry available to them. The poet using free verse must *create his own form*. In this way, form becomes as original and imaginative a part of the poetic process as imagery. It is therefore impossible to make any generalizations about free verse other than to state the obvious: given this freedom, all manner of effects are possible. If this seems depressingly vague for the student, he really has to consider only one basic question when confronting a free verse poem: why has the poet chosen to create this particular form in this particular poem? Because the form of his poem will have occupied the poet to a considerable extent, tackling this one question will lead to important observations as to what the poem as a whole is trying to achieve.

Many students assume it is easier to write in free verse. This is not necessarily so. It requires great discipline and effort if its "freedom" is not to be abused. It is all too easy for free verse to become clever or gimmicky, self-conscious or self-indulgent. To illustrate the potential of the form, here are two examples from D.H. Lawrence — a poet who became a leading exponent of free verse early in the twentieth-century. In 'Snake', the poet comes across a dangerous reptile in Sicily and is torn between admiration for its primeval beauty and majesty and a conventional inner voice that tells him to destroy a menace. In the end he compromises and half-heartedly throws a log at the snake, causing it to escape quickly into a black hole. Instantly he regrets such a trivial act and the poem closes with an empty feeling of regret and self-contempt:

> For he seemed to me like a king,
> Like a king in exile, uncrowned in the underworld,
> Now due to be crowned again.
>
> And so, I missed my chance with one of the lords
> Of life.
> And I have something to expiate:
> A pettiness.

The longer, flowing lines recall the descriptions of the snake's splendour earlier in the poem. Then comes the break and pause, as we feel the poet contemplating his mean deed, followed by the short, dull, quiet lines of the ending, that particularly emphasize the feeling of "pettiness".

In 'The Ship of Death', one of the last poems Lawrence wrote, the dying poet contemplates the journey into eternity:

> There is no port, there is nowhere to go
> only the deepening blackness darkening still
> blacker upon the soundless, ungurgling flood
> darkness at one with darkness, up and down

26 · FORM

and sideways utterly dark, so there is no direction any more
and the little ship is there; yet she is gone.
She is not seen, for there is nothing to see her by.
She is gone! gone! and yet
somewhere she is there.
Nowhere!

What impresses here is how the poet utilises free verse for some remark-able rhythmic effects. The occasional absence of commas (as in lines 1–3) and the lines that flow almost like a torrent into the following lines (lines 1–6) provide a vivid impression of encircling darkness and chaos. Yet the poet's control of the rhythm and form he is using also suggest an impression of underlying harmony and unity, in spite of the seeming chaos — an impression crucial to the poem's meaning and the poet's belief. Given the poem's highly-charged and deeply-moving emotional and spiritual content — and these come through particularly in the use of exclamation and shorter lines, where a bleak, sparse line like 'Nowhere!' contrasts effectively with the crowded earlier lines, it is a tes-timony to the poet's discipline and control of form that the communica-tion of his state of mind, heart and soul at this most intense of moments never becomes excessive or unintelligibly meaningless.

Sonnet

A sonnet has fourteen lines and is almost invariably written in ambic pentameter. There are two distinct types of sonnet in English poetry — the *Petrarchan* and the *Shakespearean*. It is a form of poetry that was most popular during Elizabethan times, where it was usually used for love poetry. Although its usage has declined, poets have continued to explore the potential of the sonnet as a poetic form. Its importance is assured for the simple reason that some of the finest poems in English are sonnets.

Petrarchan sonnets: These poems take their name from the fourteenth-century Italian poet, Petrarch. Here the fourteen lines are divided into two basic units — the first, of eight lines, known as the *octave*; and the second, of six lines, known as the *sestet*. The sonnet makes intricate and complex use of rhyme. In the Petrarchan octave, the pattern of rhyme, or *rhyme scheme* as it is called, is usually *abba abba*. This is the normal method of representing the rhyme scheme of a poem: *a* represents the sound at the end of the first line and any subsequent lines that rhyme with that sound are also represented by *a*; when a different sound is introduced, it is represented by *b* and any lines that rhyme with that sound will also be represented by *b*; each new sound introduced takes the following letter of the alphabet as its representation. Thus *abba* represents the first four lines, in which line one rhymes with line four and line two with line three. In the octave, the pattern is repeated, using the same sounds. (If the pattern was the same but the sounds different, it would read *cddc*.) In the sestet several rhyme schemes are possible — *cdcdcd* (the most common), or *cdecde*, or *cdedce*.

As an example, here is 'Remember', by Christina Rossetti:

> Remember me when I am gone away,
>> Gone far away into the silent land;
>> When you can no more hold me by the hand,
> Nor I half turn to go yet turning stay.
> Remember me when no more day by day
>> You tell me of our future you have planned:
>> Only remember me; you understand
> It will be late to counsel then or pray.
> Yet if you should forget me for a while
>> And afterwards remember, do not grieve:
>> For if the darkness and corruption leave
>> A vestige of the thoughts that once I had,
> Better by far you should forget and smile
>> Than that you should remember and be sad.

Here we have a fourteen-line poem, with lines of ten syllables, divided into an octave and a sestet — in other words, a Petrarchan sonnet. Using our rhyme scheme 'short-hand', we can indicate the rhyme scheme of the octave as *abba abba* and that of the sestet as *cdd ece*. The basic point about this form of poetry is that the octave/sestet division, together with the rhyme scheme, provide a distinct break almost in the middle of the poem (i.e. after line eight). Therefore, if what the poet has to say can be contained within this compact unit of fourteen lines and if part of the intention is to convey a certain shift in thought or feeling or perspective, the Petrarchan sonnet offers him many possibilities. In the example quoted, the poet is asking to be remembered by a loved one after she has gone 'into the silent land' — presumably died. However, almost as an afterthought, she realizes her love for this person is such that she does not wish to cause any grieving, so if thinking of their past relationship should in any way make that person sad, it is better they 'forget and smile'. The poet uses the form of the Petrarchan sonnet to suggest this change in thought and feeling. (The key to this shift lies in the word "Yet".)

This break, then, or shift in emphasis, is a main characteristic of the Petrarchan sonnet, though inevitably not all poets use it in this way. Milton, for instance, was one poet to write such sonnets and continue the sense and feeling unbroken through the fourteen lines. The feeling of self-contained neatness, of compact integration of meaning that this shorter form of poetry can bring, still remains however.

Shakespearean sonnets: This is characterized by its couplet ending —
i.e. two consecutive lines that rhyme. It can still comprise an octave and
sestet, though it perhaps falls more naturally into three groups of four
lines and the concluding couplet. The rhyme scheme is usually *abab cdcd
efef gg*, although this is frequently varied. Let us take a famous example
from the poet who has given his name to this sonnet variation (Sonnet
XVIII):

> Shall I compare thee to a Summer's day?
> Thou art more lovely and more temperate:
> Rough winds do shake the darling buds of May,
> And Summer's lease hath all too short a date:
> Sometime too hot the eye of heaven shines,
> And often is his gold complexion dimm'd,
> And every fair from fair some-time declines,
> By chance, or nature's changing course untrim'd:
> But thy eternal Summer shall not fade,
> Nor lose possession of that fair thou ow'st,
> Nor shall death brag thou wandr'st in his shade,
> When in eternal lines to time thou grow'st,
> > So long as men can breathe or eyes can see,
> > So long lives this, and this gives life to thee.

The typical effect — the decisive emphasis and air of pronounced finality
— lies in the concluding couplet. This can appear as a resounding proclamation, a confident conclusion to the poet's argument, or as an unexpected, 'sting in the tail' type twist. Here the poet has been elevating the
beauty of the person addressed, seeing it as superior to the beauty of Nature. It is superior not only in quality, but also in the fact that it will live
forever because it has been immortalized in poetry and will, therefore, be
perceived and appreciated as long as 'men can breathe or eyes can see'.
This is the point that is delivered in the poem's quietly triumphant, final
assertion in the couplet.

The sonnet is often seen as the most poetic of all forms of poetry. This
has something to do with its traditional associations with love — that
most classically perennial theme of poetry. However, it also relates to the
delicate musical potential of the sonnet — a potential that lies in its brevity, its varied, often elaborate rhyme schemes and its possible variation
of rhythm and tone.

Quatrains

This is a form of poetry that divides the verse into *separate stanzas of four
lines*. It is also a form of poetry that uses rhyme, and the usual rhyme
scheme for a quatrain stanza is *abab* or *abcb*. Again it is helpful to dif-
ferentiate between two types of quatrain — the *ballad* form and the *heroic*
quatrain.

Ballad Quatrains: Quatrains tend to move quite lightly and quickly in the ballad form, in the use of shorter line length and rhyme. They also create a natural pause in the break between stanzas. For these reasons it is suitable for narrative poetry (i.e. poetry that tells a story). The flowing movement helps prevent monotony, while the pauses help the poet to vary the pace or tone, or shift the narrative emphasis. The original *folk ballads*, which were usually sung, were a long-established tradition. Later poets, notably Wordsworth and Coleridge (who produced a seminal collection of poems together, called the *Lyrical Ballads*), developed the form along more sophisticated, literary lines, while seeking to preserve something of the simplicity and directness of the older ballads. The shorter lines of the ballad quatrain usually consist of a line of eight syllables (that will have four stressed syllables) followed by a slightly shorter line (containing three stressed syllables), as in Keats' 'La Belle Dame Sans Merci':

> I met a lady in the Meads,
>> Full beautiful, a fairy's child,
> Her hair was long, her foot was light
>> And her eyes were wild.
>
> I made a garland for her head,
>> And bracelets too, and fragrant Zone;
> She looked at me as she did love
>> And made sweet moan.

Even from a short extract, we can sense how the flow of such poetry lends itself to story-telling. The rhyming is full (in the sense of exact repetition of sound in the rhymes) and one-syllable — a light, quick form of rhyme. The shorter lines, at the end of each stanza, arrest the attention and the following "pause" allows us to dwell and ponder on what has just been said.

Heroic Quatrain: As the student should now be more familiar with our concept of heroic, he can begin to imagine how this form of quatrain will differ from the previous one. Its themes tend to be the more serious or profound issues of philosophy, religion, history etc., while its style is more grand and elevated. The lightness of touch of the ballad would not be completely suitable. Ballads tend to deal with deliberately simple, homely, or rustic characters and situations. Yet poets who preferred the loftier, heroic manner still wished to explore the possibilities of the quatrain. Quatrains were, therefore, developed in which the lines were lengthened to straightforward iambic pentameter, so that poets wishing to deal with an issue, or series of issues, in an involved, protracted manner and who wanted to use the potential of rhyme without being bound by the rigid rhyme scheme of couplets, had an alternative to both blank verse and heroic couplets. One of the best examples of such poetry is Gray's 'Elegy Written in a Country Church Yard', where the poet looks at the graves of simple, poor country folk and is led to philosophical contemplation:

> Let not Ambition mock their useful Toil,
> Their homely Joys and Destiny obscure;
> Nor Grandeur hear with a disdainful Smile,
> The short and simple Annals of the Poor.
> The Boast of Heraldry, the Pomp of Power,
> And all that Beauty, all that Wealth e'er gave,
> Awaits alike th' inevitable Hour,
> The Paths of Glory lead but to the Grave.

Students may come across slight variations of these two patterns of quatrain — the most likely being one that lies somewhere between the two. Here the lines have eight syllables (or four 'feet' and known as *tetrameters* as opposed to the five 'feet' of *pentameters*) and the rhyme scheme is usually *abba*. This is found in Tennyson's 'In Memoriam':

> And was the day of my delight
> As pure and perfect as I say?
> The very source and fount of day
> Is dashed with wandering isles of night.

Given such variations (and we can notice how the Gray's 'Elegy' quoted above, for instance, does not technically divide its four line units into separate stanzas) the student will still be able to draw upon his knowledge of the form and adapt it to the poem in question. Quite often, any deviation from the standard pattern of the form being used will provide a telling insight into what exactly it is the poet is trying to achieve.

These, then, are the main forms of English poetry. A brief word remains on some of the others a student may come across. These are less common and, in the case of the first two, much more difficult to define.

Lyrics

Lyrics were originally intended to be sung — we still use the term to indicate the words of a song. There is no set form for lyric poetry in English. They are usually short poems intended to express an intense reaction to a particular person, thing or situation — most commonly an aspect of natural beauty. It is poetry that usually conveys an emotional, spontaneous feeling in a light and delicate manner. It was a form of poetry, with its sophisticated and courtly associations, that was very much in vogue in Chaucer's time — mainly through the heavy French influence on English culture that followed the Norman invasion and conquest of King William. The only other times it received sustained poetic attention were during the Elizabethan and Romantic periods. One example will serve to illustrate the lyric's essential qualities; this is the 'Love Song' from Beaumont and Fletcher's *Valentinian*:

> Now the lustry Spring is seen,
>   Golden yellow, gaudy Blue,
>   Daintily invite the view.
> Every where, on every Green,
> Roses blushing as they blow,
>   And enticing men to pull,
> Lilies whither than the snow,
>   Woodbines of sweet honey full.
>   All Love's Emblems and all cry,
>   Ladies, if not pluck't we die.

The short lines, the light, delicate rhyme with its neatly concluding couplet are typical of the lyric's bright, flowing musical quality.

Odes

Again there is no set structure for this form of poetry. (The complexities of Pindaric and Horatian odes need not concern the Advanced Level student.) As with the lyric, it is characterized more by the type of poetry produced than by any identifiable form. Basically, an ode is an elaborate address to, or celebration of, a person, or place, or situation. The Romantic poets particularly were concerned with developing the ode — indeed its continued importance as a form of poetry has been guaranteed by some of the fine odes they produced. For the Romantic poets, most notably Keats and Wordsworth, this development consisted in using the ode as a poetic form for philosophical contemplation.

Odes tend to be serious in subject matter and elevated in style. Line length and stanza structuring tend to be elaborate and irregular. It is often seen as a longer form of lyric poetry and certainly, at times, an ode may have such delicate, lyrical quality. In Wordsworth's famous 'Ode: Intimations of Immortality' we find:

> The Rainbow comes and goes,
> And lovely is the Rose,
> The Moon doth with delight
> Look round her when the heavens are bare,
> Waters on a starry night
> Are beautiful and fair;
> The sunshine is a glorious birth;
> But yet I know, where'er I go,
> That there hath passed away a glory from the earth.

Yet, whereas the lyric quoted above from Beaumont and Fletcher represents half the entire poem, the stanza from Wordsworth is just one of eleven — and the shortest one at that. The longest has thirty-nine lines — and a more irregular number for line and rhyme patterning is difficult to imagine. We can sense the more serious, weighty intention of the ode in the poem's conclusion. The poet has been meditating on the very meaning of our existence and our relationship with Nature — a typical Romantic theme for the ode, as the very title here indicates. The poem has moved through agonies of doubt and confusion towards a reconciliation of the problems that have tormented the poet. To celebrate this fact and help elevate the feeling at the poem's conclusion, the poem moves into iambic pentameter:

> Thanks to the human heart by which we live,
> Thanks to its tenderness, its joys, and fears,
> To me the meanest flower that blows can give
> Thoughts that do often lie too deep for tears.

Other Forms

There are two other forms to be mentioned in conclusion. One uses iambic pentameter, and has four variations. The first has stanzas of eight lines, with a usual rhyme scheme of *abababcc*, and is called *Ottava Rima*. The most famous example of this form of poetry is Byron's *Don Juan*. Our example probably contains the most outrageous rhyme in the whole of English poetry in its concluding couplet:

> 'Tis pity learned virgins ever wed
>> With persons of no sort of education,
> Or gentlemen, who, though well born and bred,
>> Grow tired of scientific conversation:
> I don't choose to say much upon this head,
>> I'm a plain man and in a single station,
> But — Oh! ye lords of ladies intellectual,
> Inform us truly, have they not henpecked you all?

The second variation on this form has stanzas of seven lines and a usual rhyme scheme of *ababbcc*. This is called *Rhyme Royal* — a form employed by Chaucer in *Troilus and Cressida*. A third variation came from the poet Spenser and carries his name — *Spenserian Stanza*. This has nine lines, with a rhyme scheme of *ababbcbcc*. The final variation has six lines and is, in effect, a quatrain with a couplet — i.e. *ababcc*. These variations around the same basic form tend to develop the characteristics of heroic quatrains, combined with the additional, pointed emphasis or neat finality of the concluding couplet. This provides considerable scope for effects of humour and surprise. Such poems tend to seek an ironic, or sophisticated, or 'tongue-in-cheek' effect and rarely seek a direct emotional involvement or response from the reader, although some modern poems have experimented with these forms, particularly the six-line stanza, for more emotional, even tragic, purposes.

The final form is poetry written in *Tercets*. These divide the verse into stanzas of three lines. This is not a common form of poetry, yet again it is a form that has occasionally attracted some modern poets. Line length in the tercet may be regular or varied. The tercet may have one rhyme, as in Shelley's:

> O wild West Wind, thou breath of Autumn's being,
> Thou, from whose unseen presence the leaves dead
> Are driven, like ghosts from an enchanter fleeing,

or complete rhyme, as in Andrew Young's:

> I see you did not try to save
> The bouquet of white flowers I gave;
> So fast they wither on your grave,

or no rhyme at all, as in Sylvia Plath's:

> Knifelike, he was chaste enough,
> Pure death's-metal. The yardman's
> Flung brick perfected his laugh.

If the tercets are interlinked by rhyme — i.e. *aba bcb cdc ded* — a pattern that produces flowing, intricate continuity, the form is known as *Terza Rima*. The student will have to evaluate the specific effect of tercets in a given instance, observing whether the verse flows freely through the stanzas or whether it is segmented in short, separate, self-contained, three-line units.

FORM AND THE REFERENCE POEMS

Poem A   Poem A is written in quatrains — technically heroic quatrains (i.e. four-line stanzas and lines of iambic pentameter that rhyme alternately). The use of the longer-lined quatrain form has a slower natural rhythm that is more suited to philosophical or contemplative poetry. We might add, however, that there is a delicate, lighter quality here that is reminiscent of the shorter quatrain form, or even the lyric. The use of short, separate stanzas allows the poet to make a specific point or present an image, and then pause to allow the reader to ponder the implications.

Poem B   Poem B uses free verse for several reasons. Because it is a far less formal or heightened form of poetry, it enables the poet to convey the deliberately 'low key', casually intimate feeling that is so central to the poem. The poet also uses the freedom to arrange his own line-length for rhythmic effects that emphasize key words or ideas.

Poem C   Poem C consciously adopts the style, tone and form of the type of heroic couplets the great Augustan poets used to write. This highly-structured form conveys the opposite feeling to the previous one and is deliberately formal and elevated, to lend weight and substance to its pronouncements. It also uses rhyming couplets for precision and balance. This tends to impress the reader with a sense of sophisticated intelligence, and therefore credibility, on the poet's part — much as with the poetry of Dryden and Pope. It also emphasizes the irony and humour of the verse (lines 7–8, or 19–20).

Poem D Poem D is a sonnet. Technically it is a Shakespearean sonnet and as such it makes full use of the concluding couplet for its resounding, triumphant ending. However, it does not follow the traditional units of octave/sestet or four line groupings, as the sense of the poem moves through such conventional breaks. This slightly original development is appropriate enough for a poem in praise of a man credited with a major development of the sonnet form.

Poem E Poem E is an ode. It is conventional in the sense that it is a celebratory poem, specifically addressed to the object of its praise. It also has the lilting, lyrical quality of many odes. Its structuring of line and stanza length, and also its rhyme scheme are perhaps unusually regular throughout. This is perfectly in keeping with the calmness and serenity that the poem seeks to convey about autumn.

CHAPTER 6

T O N E

The first impressions we receive on meeting a person for the first time relate to the person's physical appearance and tone of voice. These are the first things that say something about that person, even though they may, at times, be misleading. It is similar with a poem. Having observed its physical appearance, or layout (i.e. its form), the first impressions we gather from our reading will concern the poem's *tone*.

Tone, in poetry, can refer to the tone the poet adopts towards his reader, as well as the tone he displays towards his theme or subject. If we are sensitive to the poet's tone, we begin to understand the way the poet feels about what he is writing and we therefore have an invaluable aid when it comes to assessing the intention behind the poem and what the poet is really trying to achieve. We can describe a poem's tone by means of the type of adjective used to describe 'tones of voice'. Towards the reader, the poet may adopt a tone that is aggressive, confiding, subservient, cajoling, sarcastic etc. As it relates to the theme, or presentation of the subject-matter, the tone may be wistful, admiring, pensive, harsh etc. The poet's attitude to the reader may be neutral, as in reference Poem E, where no discernible tone relates to the reader. The prevailing tone in such poems will relate exclusively to the theme.

A poem will demand to be read in a certain tone. The student could ask himself how he would imagine the poet would read the poem if he were present to do so. What tone would be detected in his voice? The tone may also shift, or change, within the course of a poem. The reason for it doing so will again highlight an important aspect of the poem. A student's sensitivity to a poem's tone will depend on his ability to 'hear' the poem in his mind. Once more, as much practice as possible in reading poetry out loud and exposing oneself to listening to poetry read by experienced, perhaps professional, readers will help develop this facility, especially for the non-native student of English poetry.

TONE AND ATMOSPHERE

Many students have difficulty differentiating between *tone* and *atmosphere* in poetry. The atmosphere in a poem is the prevailing mood, an attempt by the poet to make the *reader* feel or react in a certain way towards the theme, whereas the tone tells us how the *poet* feels. The two are closely related and frequently similar, yet the atmosphere created in a poem is more directly related to the poem's use of imagery. If the tone of a poem is wistful, or yearning, the atmosphere will probably be appropriately sad, or melancholic, perhaps nostalgic. However, tone and atmosphere may, at times, be different, perhaps 'played against' one another, for a particular effect. Several modern poets, notably Jon Silkin and Dylan Thomas, for instance, have written poems on the tragic deaths of young children. By adopting tones that are deliberately un-emotional, almost to the point of being matter-of-fact, even cold, they achieve an atmosphere of sadness and melancholy that is, perhaps, far more effective than that of similar poems that treat the theme in a more emotional, sentimental tone.

To take one further example, not actually from a poem, but certainly poetic in the wider sense of the word, we may consider the famous trial scene arranged by the "mad" king in Act IV of *King Lear*. In this scene, King Lear arraigns and 'tries' the daughters who have treated him so shamefully. The tone here ranges from the whimsical to bitter anger. Yet because of all that has gone before, and because this charade is played out in a decrepit hut before the ragged remnants of the king's court — an old man, a 'fool' and a 'lunatic' — the prevailing atmosphere is hopelessly sad and shatteringly desolate. This impact is deepened all the more by the tone of the oblivious king.

The fundamental point about tone and atmosphere is that they should, in some way, be complementary, combining together for an overall effect, even if their specific qualities are distinct and different.

TONE AND THE REFERENCE POEMS

Poem A   In this poem, the opening word — 'We' — and its constant repetition create an intimate tone. It suggests a bond between the poet and the reader, a sense that we share the same fate, as the reader is drawn into the scope of the poem. The general tone as the poem progresses is one of calm assurance. The contemplative, philosophical manner leads to quietly confident assertions, especially in the concluding lines. The delicate images of beauty in the first two stanzas are not allowed to transport us. We do not get carried away with their momentary splendour as the tone restrains us with a sense of 'in spite of all this'. The tone in this poem suggests a mind that has thought long and deeply about what it has to say. We tend to feel it is a mind we can respect and trust.

Poem B   The tone here is also intimate, yet in a far more informal manner. It is conversational, especially in its opening. We feel we are listening to a voice speaking to us directly, treating us as equals, almost as acquaintances. Again, this draws the reader into the poem, though more subtly than in Poem A. What the poem has to say will therefore relate to us. In keeping with this, the tone is also strikingly colloquial, especially in such lines as:

> Where dogs go on with their doggy life and the torturer's horse
> Scratches its innocent behind on a tree.

As we move more deeply into implications of this poem, we will see just how crucial this casual, low-key use of tone is to the poem as a whole.

Poem C   Poem C reveals a device sometimes employed by poets where the tone deliberately creates a role for the poet as he pretends to adopt a position, usually ironically, that is extreme, or even the opposite of what he really believes. Swift's 'Modest Proposal', although not a poem, is a marvellous example of such a use of tone; in this piece, Swift "adopts" the role of a deep-thinking social reformer, utterly plausible, persuasive and rational in his tone, to state he has a solution to the problems of famine, starvation and infant mortality in Ireland — which is to *eat* the young children. Swift adopts this tone and position to highlight the callous indifference to such problems of those who are in a position to offer *genuine* help. The poet in Poem C is doing something similar. Because he feels his concept of 'story-telling' (i.e. writing in general), when it comes to fiction, will be regarded as extreme or controversial, he offers his views under the guise of 'Devil's Advice'. Again there is a feeling that we are being addressed directly. The tone here though has an air of sententious authority, as the principles are laid down as if they were the Ten Commandments. As the poet adopts the tone of a public lecture towards his audience, the tone within the poem itself alternates subtly between ironic semi-seriousness and positive statement, both aptly captured in such lines as:

> Sigh then, or frown, but leave (as in despair)
> Motive and end and moral in the air.

Poem D   Poem D directly addresses its subject, William Shakespeare. This is a common practice in English poetry ('odes to', 'hymns to', 'in memoria' etc.). Such poems are usually elevated and admiring in tone — Dryden and Pope again being notable exceptions. In this poem, the reader is again 'embraced' and involved by the use of 'we' and 'our'.

There is a sense of awe when the poet speaks of Shakespeare ('Didst tread on earth unguessed at') which is contrasted with a tone of self-deprecating (almost contemptuous) humility when the poet talks of us 'lesser mortals' ('foiled searching of morality'). If we are sensitive to this duality of tone here it will lead us to the poem's central issue: the difference between Shakespeare's achievement and that of others, and what it can mean for us.

Poem E   Another example of direct address is provided by Poem E. The idea of addressing Nature, in one aspect or another, may be a well-worn, almost clichéd, poetic device, yet here we have a most subtle and satisfying example of such poetry. The tone is one of quiet, yet profound admiration. The feeling of delight and awe is controlled and refined, as mellow and serene as the poet's perception of the season he is describing. Yet there are still moments when the feeling becomes more wondering, more emotional, as in:

> to set budding more
> And still more, later flowers for the bees,
> Until they think warm days will never cease ...

EXERCISES

1. People always make war when they say they love peace.
    The loud love of peace makes one quiver more than any battle-cry.
    Why should one love peace? it is so obviously vile to make war.
    Loud peace propaganda makes war seem imminent.
    It is a form of war, even, self-assertion and being wise for other people.
    Let people be wise for themselves.

    a. What is the 'tone' of this extract?
    b. What is the poet's attitude to 'people'?
    c. Whom do you think the poet is criticizing?

2. Death, be not proud, though some have called thee
    Mighty and dreadful, for thou art not so:
    For those whom thou think'st thou dost overthrow
    Die not, poor Death.

    a. What is the poet's 'tone' and attitude towards death?
    b. Which words best convey this attitude?

3. 'Tis hard to say, if greater want of skill
    Appear in writing or in judging ill;
    But of the two, less dang'rous is th'offence
    To tire our patience, than mislead our sense.
    Some few in that, but numbers err in this,
    Ten censure wrong for one who writes amiss;
    A fool might once himself alone expose,
    Now one in verse makes many more in prose.

a. This extract compares bad poets with bad critics. How does 'tone'
    convey the poet's attitude to bad critics?

4. Say not the struggle nought availeth,
        The labour and the wounds are vain,
    The enemy faints not, nor faileth,
        And as things have been they remain.

a. What tone does the poet adopt here towards his reader?

5. Nor dread nor hope attend
    A dying animal;
    A man awaits his end
    Dreading and hoping all;
    Many times he died,
    Many times rose again ....
    ... He knows death to the bone —
    Man has created death.

a. What is the poet's 'tone' here?
b. What is his attitude to man's fear of death?

6. I never saw a wild thing
    sorry for itself.
    A small bird will drop frozen dead from a bough
    without ever having felt sorry for itself.

a. What is the implied attitude to mankind here?
b. How does it compare with that of No. 5?

CHAPTER 7

I M A G E R Y

NATURE AND FUNCTION

This is probably the single most vexing aspect of poetry appreciation. Many students struggle through their course without ever feeling confident that they really understand the nature or function of imagery, while at the same time realizing it is the central characteristic of poetic writing.

Simply put, imagery attempts to make the communication more vivid, more immediate, or more exact. An image should help us see, or feel, or hear, or focus our thought, more clearly and sharply on what the poet is trying to convey or describe. Its function is basically descriptive, yet in a deep sense of the word, as it does not seek to give simple, factual or phsyical representations, but more to evoke *feelings* in the reader and *atmosphere* within the poem. It tells us much about how the poet feels towards what he is describing and how he wants us to feel. The reader cannot be passive towards imagery; it forces him to respond in some way, to use his mind, his senses, his emotions, his imagination. It is subjective in that it tells us the poet's feelings — and two poems on the same theme will use different images to convey the different ways the poets feel about the subject — and in that our response to it will be our own response. If we have read a poem closely and sensitively, we should, no doubt, feel in a certain way towards it, a way others giving the poem a similar reading will probably share. Yet most of the (often valid) disagreements about what a poem, or part of a poem, means, together with most of the misreadings or misinterpretations of poetry, stem from the way we perceive imagery in the poem.

An analogy from the visual arts may usefully help to highlight the function of imagery if we think of the difference between photography — and I am here referring to the snap-shot type of photography of the occasional photographer — and painting. Such a photograph tries, as faithfully and realistically as possible, to capture the scene or person before the camera. A painter, with his use of texture, tone and colour, tries to say something about the person or scene he paints — either how he feels towards his subject, or what he perceives as its essence or character. He does not simply copy or represent — he wants to communicate a *feeling* about the subject in some way or other. This is perhaps most obvious if we think of some of the more extreme forms of modern art where there is no clear, or immediately identifiable, subject in view. Yet even more traditional portrait painters, such as Rubens and Gainsborough, are as much concerned with communicating a feeling about their subject as with giving an accurate representation of the physical characteristics. The analogy cannot be pushed too far. Modern developments in photography have been creative and artistic and do, in fact, say something about the subject. But, in general, the example serves to focus on how imagery in poetry works like tone, texture, colour, etc. in painting.

Imagery is a lot less specialized or rare than many students suppose. We all use it, almost unconsciously, every day. Simple phrases such as 'he droned on and on', or 'quick as a flash', or 'she's got a few screws loose', are all technically images. In other words, imagery covers any usage of language that is *figurative* — i.e. where the words used are not to be taken literally, in the sense of their dictionary definition. As such, it embraces all uses of metaphor, simile, figures of speech, etc. In our examples above, only certain types of flying insects may be literally said to 'drone', yet in the phrase 'he droned on and on' it is applied figuratively, because of its associations of sound and because of the long, drawn out vowel sound, to give a more *vivid* impression of how boring and monotonous the speaker was. Literally speaking, only electricity or certain combustible chemicals can 'flash' — yet the word may be used figuratively to give an impression of blinding speed. With 'she's got a few screws loose', unless the lady in question happens to be a robot, we have another image to indicate, strikingly and humorously, that someone is behaving in an illogical, irrational, or abnormal manner.

TYPES OF IMAGERY

For the convenience of analysis, we can outline different types of imagery.

Visual Imagery

Obviously, this form of imagery helps us to see, or visualize, what is being described. A visual image will always do more than simply provide a physical description. For instance, a reference book will tell us that a 'gentian' is 'a plant that usually has blue leaves'. Compare this with the description of D.H. Lawrence, in his poem 'Bavarian Gentians':

> Bavarian gentians, big and dark, only dark
> darkening the daytime torchlike with the smoking blueness of
> Pluto's gloom,
> ribbed and torchlike, with their blaze of darkness spreading blue
> ...

The poet is not just describing. He has been moved by the striking, mysterious beauty in the form and colouring of the plant and wants to convey that feeling. His images are so compelling however, ('smoking blueness', 'Pluto's gloom', 'blaze of darkness') that we also receive a vivid impression of the gentian's physical qualities.

Aural Imagery

This is imagery that enables us to 'hear' what is being described. It is less common than visual imagery, which is abundant in all poetry, yet can be used to telling effect. In Wilfred Owen's poem, 'Anthem for Doomed Youth', we find:

> Only the stuttering rifles rapid rattle
> Can patter out their hasty orisons.

Here the use of *t* and *r* sounds, together with the grouping of short, harsh vowel sounds, effectively suggests the gunfire, especially machine-gun-fire, of a World War I battle.

Tactile Imagery

This form of imagery appeals to our sense of touch. It attempts to communicate the sensation of physically feeling something. In Coleridge's 'Ancient Mariner', tactile imagery helps us to 'share' the parched sensation of thirst that the becalmed sailors are suffering:

> And every tongue, through utter drought,
> Was withered at the root;
> We could not speak, no more than if
> We had been choked with soot.

The effect is achieved mainly by the final image 'choked with soot' but also by the repetition of the harsh, dry *k* sound ('*C*ould', 'spea*k*', 'cho*k*ed'), which is actually produced back in the throat, where thirst affects us.

There are no common terms for the rare examples of images of taste and smell. Such personalised sensations are difficult to convey. They do occur, however. Keats comes close to succeeding in the 'Eve of St. Agnes', where he attempts images of taste:

With jellies soother than the creamy curd,
And lucent syrups, tinct with cinnamon;
Manna and dates, in argosy transferred
From Fez; and spiced dainties, every one,
From silken Samarcand to cedared Lebanon ...

However, the impressions here are effective largely through visual ('lucent') and tactile ('soother', 'silken') details and through exotic association ('Fez', 'Samarcand'), rather than actual images of taste. In the same poem, he also tries to convey images of smell:

... perplexed she lay
Until the poppied warmth of sleep oppressed
Her soothed limbs ...

Here the vowel sounds are appropriately heavy and 'sleepy', yet such imagery is difficult and poets are usually left talking in such a way about the 'drowsy fumes' of poppies and such like (as in Reference Poem E) and leaving most of the work to the reader's imagination.

In this general survey of imagery, we may look at other elements, often termed 'figures of speech', which are specific devices in their own right, yet which relate to imagery as a whole.

Metaphor

This is when a word is made to 'stand for' something different from its usual, literal meaning. In this way it is an implied comparison between the two things being related — i.e. the normal meaning or association of the word and that which it is made to represent in this specific instance. It is an 'implied' comparison because it does not use the words 'like' or 'as' — which is a more direct form of comparison. In the opening lines of G.M. Hopkins 'The Windhover', the poet celebrates the bird's beauty with exaggerated, almost breathless praise:

I caught this morning morning's minion, king-
    dom of daylight's dauphin, dapple-dawn-drawn Falcon ...

The bird is seen as the 'minion', or darling, of the morning. Thus the normal associations of 'minion' are related to the bird and because of this metaphor we learn how the poet feels towards what he is describing. Similarly, in calling the bird the dauphin, or 'heir', of the 'kingdom of daylight' the metaphor conveys both an impression of the bird and its beauty in the early morning sunlight, as well as the poet's feelings. The effect of metaphor is 'concentrated' — which sometimes makes its meaning difficult to unravel. We can sense the loss of intensity if the poet had written 'like the minion of morning', or 'like the dauphin of the kingdom of daylight'.

Simile

Sometimes the poet will feel it is more appropriate to make a comparison and actually use 'like' or 'as'. This is called a simile. There is a poem by W.B. Yeats called 'Long-legged Fly', in which the poet describes the mystical, trance-like concentration used by those who have made decisions that have profoundly affected history or culture. He imagines Caesar considering whether or not to cross the Rubicon stream with his army (and thereby violate state orders and bring about civil war — a war that was eventually to elevate Caesar to complete power in Rome), or Michelangelo, contemplating his design for the Sistine Chapel, a work that profoundly influenced concepts in Art, and writes:

> Like a long-legged fly upon the stream
> His mind moves upon silence.

The simile is perhaps less intense than the metaphor, yet that does not mean it is in any way an inferior device. One cannot imagine the refrain from Yeats just quoted having the same impact if it was written any other way — as a metaphor perhaps. It is simply a matter of the poet deciding which device is the most effective for his present purpose.

Alliteration

This refers to the repetition of the same consonant sound, usually at the beginning of each word, within a series of words. As such, it is a device of 'sound' and is therefore a part of aural imagery. Again it must be emphasized that 'spotting' the device and naming it is not enough. The student must comment on the effect a particular instance of alliteration brings to the specific poem. All the consonant sounds may be alliterated and by no means do they produce the same effect. Some may be light and flowing ('l's, 'r's), others harsh and grating ('k's, 'g's). Some are heavily emphatic (the so-called 'plosive' consonants, 'b', 'p', 't', 'd'). The student will still have to perceive the type of effect of the example before him, as certain sounds, like 's', may be soft and gentle or hissing and menacing. Tennyson, in 'In Memoriam', uses the 's' alliteration to convey the lulling sound of waves on a calm sea:

> Calm on the seas, and silver sleep,
> And waves that sway themselves in rest ...

Onomatopoeia

This word, along with its dread spelling (the adjective is *onomatopoeic*), indicates another aural device. It refers to words that, in some way, sound like or enact their meaning. At a simple level, this is seen in such words as 'crash', 'scream' or 'stutter'. In poetry, it is usually used more subtly. In D.H. Lawrence's 'Piano', the poet recalls how as a young child, he would sit under the piano while his mother played — a position that amplified the sound quite considerably for his young ears:

> A child under the piano, in the boom of the tingling strings.

The vivid aural impression comes from the onomatopoeic 'boom' and 'tingling', which suggest the intensified sound of the bass and treble notes respectively.

Assonance

Assonance is another aural device, this time indicating a repeated vowel sound. Again a variety of effects is possible, from the light and breezy, as in the song of Autolycus in Shakespeare's *Winter's Tale*:

> The lark, that tirra-lyrra chants,
> With heigh, with heigh, the thrush and jay

to the slow and languorous, as in Gray's:

> The lowing Herd winds slowly oe'r the lea,
> The plowman homeward plods his weary way

from the 'Elegy in a Country Church Yard'.

Personification

This is when an inanimate object or abstract idea is attributed with feelings, thoughts or sensations normally associated with living creatures. This happens most frequently when aspects of Nature are seen in human terms, as in these three examples, all from Shelley:

> Swiftly walk oe'r the western wave,
> Spirit of Night

or:

> Rough wind that moanest loud ...
> ... Wail for the world's wrong

(where we see how one word, such as 'moan' or 'wail' can produce personification), and finally his famous address to the Moon, which asks if 'she' is 'pale for weariness' from 'wandering' the heavens in 'lonely' isolation.

Abstract ideas (liberty, truth, one's country etc.) are also often personified, as in Wordsworth's 'Ode to Duty' — which he characterizes as the 'Stern Daughter of the Voice of God'.

Hyperbole

This is the use of deliberate, sometimes outrageous, exaggeration. The main potential for hyperbole is obviously comic or ironic. In Marvell's 'To His Coy Mistress', the poet laments, semi-seriously, that his 'mistress' will not submit to his amorous advances. This would not be a problem, he says, if they lived forever, for then he could be more patient in his wooing and

> An hundred years should go to praise
> Thine eyes, and on they Forehead Gaze.
> Two hundred to adore each Breast:
> But thirty thousand to the rest.

However, hyperbole can be used sincerely, as genuine praise, as in Cleopatra's famous speech on her dead lover Antony, in Shakespeare's *Antony and Cleopatra*. Here she talks of him as a 'Colossus', whose 'legs bestrid the ocean'.

IMAGERY AND THE REFERENCE POEMS

Poem A   To show the transient, fragile quality of beauty, the first two stanzas of Poem A offer two delicate images. The first is from Nature, that of clouds trailing across the moon at midnight. The poem opens with a simile — 'We are as clouds' — that directly relates human existence to the image that is about to be developed. Atmosphere is quickly established by words like 'veil'. If we are trying to assess the quality or feeling an image is bringing to a poem, it is sometimes useful to substitute the more prosaic, or literal word, that would normally be used. Here it would be something like 'cover' — a word that carries none of the translucent, delicate, mysterious associations of 'veil'. This is followed by the gentle and soft alliteration of the *m* sound in 'midnight moon'.

Qualities of light and movement are brought out in the following lines:

> How restlessly they speed, and gleam, and quiver,
> Streaking the darkness radiantly!

The accumulation of verbs, all associated with inconstant, yet brilliant light, gives a sense of immediacy, of our watching their movement take place This is because they are all in the present tense. The culmination of this image of beauty lies in the two words stressed most heavily by the rhythm — 'Streaking' and 'radiantly'. The sense of movement, to suggest the fleeting changes of light as the clouds drift past the moon, is also conveyed by the repetition of short, light vowel sounds and the rhythmic use of 'and'. We are reminded of the comparison with human existence in the subtle use of personification contained in 'restlessly' (a state of mind or body possible only for living things). This image of the beauty of the moon and clouds is finally 'defeated', or counter-balanced, by the succeeding image of night and darkness 'closing round'. The word 'lost' has sad or mournful connotations that a word such as 'gone' might not suggest.

If the main quality of the imagery in stanza one is visual, then that of stanza two is mainly aural — appropriately enough, as the central image has to do with music. The stanza opens with another simile to remind us of the image's relation to the human situation, while 'forgotten' strengthens the feelings already implanted by 'lost'. There is repeated use of the *s* syllable in this stanza, and particularly in the first two lines, to suggest the dissonant 'music' which is now produced by these neglected instruments — and the lyre is one of the oldest known instruments. 'Blast' is unexpected and effective, with its onomatopoeic quality, in suggesting the noise now made by the lyre that could once produce beautiful music. This is emphasized also by the repetition of 'varying' and 'various' to convey the now random, disharmonious effect. There is an unclear, distorted and uncertain sound behind the alliteration of '*f*rail *f*rame', though the feeling is softened by '*m*ood or *m*odulation'. This provides a quiet, gentle close to the first half of the poem and prepares the way for the move from 'illustrative' images to more direct observation.

The images of the first two stanzas, showing that light becomes dark, music becomes discord, are now replaced by specific comment on the human situation, where the pattern is the same. Nothing is permanent. Even in the simple, ordinary, untroubled states of sleep or going about our daily business, our peace of mind can be overthrown. The use of 'we' again reminds us that we are all drawn within the poem's scope of reference. The occasional nightmare is menacingly personified, with its 'power to poison sleep', with an emphatic, ringing *p* alliteration to highlight the impact even more. Similarly, the poet describes the way a chance remembrance or association, or sudden fear or worry can destroy our equilibrium in: 'One wandering thought pollutes the day'. 'Wandering' effectively conveys the unexpected nature of such feelings, while 'pollutes' is a powerfully surprising image. The varying, ever-changing state of our lives is captured in the balance of:

> Embrace fond woe, or cast our cares away.

The idea that we 'embrace' our sorrow is unusual. Perhaps the poet is suggesting that once we realize the inevitably 'mutable' nature of our existence, we can see that sorrow has as much a role to play in our lives as joy. In this sense, it is sorrow that allows us to appreciate happiness — if we were happy all the time it would have no meaning or significance for us. Yet the image also suggests the way in which sorrow can envelop us with total gloom, perhaps emphasized here by the long, heavy vowel sounds of 'fond woe'. In contrast, the vowel sounds that describe the opposite state are light and short and the effect is intensified by the sharp, clipped alliteration: 'or cast our cares away'.

onvey the never-ending quality of the changes in our state of mind and heart, the poet uses the image of an open journey:

> The path of its departure still is free.

Often our sorrows so oppress us, or our joys become so intense, that we can perceive nothing else. This image reminds us that everything 'moves on', changes to something else. This is further stressed in the metaphors of 'Man's yesterday' and his 'tomorrow'. There is an ironic element in the final line, which states that the only thing that does not change is 'change' itself, an effect strengthened by the use of 'endure', which suggests strength of purpose and permanence. A word like 'last' would lose these ironic associations.

Poem B   Imagery in Poem A is used mainly to create an atmosphere that persuades us to see things in a certain light. In Poem B, it is used to make us think and focus more sharply on what the poet has to say. Its imagery is less elaborate and certainly less sensuous (appealing to, or involving, our senses). It is not until line four that we find the first use of imagery. The poet presents us with ordinary people, following mundane activities — 'eating or opening a window or just walking dully along' — activities that are pointedly insignificant yet which occur when certain individuals are experiencing an intense, personal crisis. The most urgent and consuming of these crises is death, for which the poet uses a metaphor — 'miraculous birth'. This does not imply a termination, but rather the beginning of a new phase of existence. For this reason, the aged and weary await death 'reverently' and 'passionately', yet young children who die and who are full of the active, joyful 'novelty' of life, do not 'specially want it to happen'. There is an effective image for such children:

> skating
> On a pond at the edge of the wood.

The activity of skating suggests their youthful, vital exuberance and a sense of movement is added through the enjambement effect. Yet the 'pond at the edge of the wood' offers a sense of the mysterious, even menace, at the prospect of their impending death. This is a particularly subtle image as 'skating' preserves a delicate balance between being an exhilarating, yet potentially dangerous, activity. Even the most glorified, dramatic form of death — 'martyrdom' — is seen as taking place in 'some untidy spot'. Here, the poem's central device of placing intense suffering in a setting that is extremely commonplace and 'unconcerned' with the individual's fate, receives its most effective image; the individual is 'martyred':

> Where the dogs go on with their doggy life and the torturer's horse
> Scratches its innocent behind on a tree.

In the second stanza, the emphasis shifts to a specific example,

Brueghel's painting of the Icarus legend. We do not need to know the actual painting as the poet proceeds to 'describe' it for us. This is interesting, because the painting itself constitutes a series of images. The poet is offering *his* impression of these images, so he uses 'key' or 'loaded' words to convey how he feels towards it. In other words, he does not simply describe the painting's images; he conveys them through images of his own. This can be seen when he talks of the plowman in the picture, who continues with his work, oblivious to what has happened to Icarus:

> the plowman may
> Have heard the splash, the forsaken cry,
> But for him it was not an important failure.

The key words here are 'may', 'forsaken' and 'important'. The inevitability of it all, the sense that life goes on anyway, no matter what, is contained in the description of the sun shining 'As it had to'. The poem depends heavily on the use of contrast. With impressive timing, we have a good example of this in the poem's final image of the ship sailing away from the boy dropping into the sea:

> and the expensive delicate ship that must have seen
> Something amazing, a boy falling out of the sky,
> Had somewhere to go and sailed calmly on.

The tragedy of Icarus, the 'Something amazing', is contrasted with 'expensive delicate' and 'sailed calmly on', while there is a further hint of inevitability behind the almost callous, casual vagueness of 'somewhere to go'.

Poem C   Similarly in Poem C the imagery engages our mind rather than our feelings or senses. The very title conjures up comic and ironic associations. The approach of the poem is to offer advice in a conventional manner of clear-cut instructions, peppered with occasional references for illustration or persuasion. Again there is use of contrast, this time between the concept of 'realistic story-telling' and the more imaginative, purely fictional concepts of the 'devil'/poet. The poet's bias in favour of his own argument lies in the contempt with which he summarizes the 'realistic' approach:

> But my advice to story-tellers is:
> Weigh out no gross of probabilities.

The subtle persuasion lies in the use of 'loaded' terms — so much so that in the following lines we accept the inversion of 'diligent' and 'known', where words usually used in a positive sense become negative faults:

> Nor yet make diligent transcription of
> Known instances of virtue, crime or love.

This reversing of standard virtues is central to the poem's progress and has already been established in the poem's ironic title.

The true artist is told to 'forge' a creation that will 'pass for true' and to do 'conscientiously what liars do'. A crucial distinction is introduced at this point between, ironically, 'false' liars (i.e. those who 'steal' or, in a literary context, plagiarize, the ideas of others) and imaginative, creative 'born' liars, who 'make things up' out of nothing. Again, there is a marked tone of contempt behind the image that describes the 'false' liars:

> the lesser sort that raid
> The mouths of others for their stock-in-trade.

We might note here how the type of writer, or story-teller, the poet 'dismisses' is seen in terms of the small-time, profit-obsessed, shopkeeper mentality — 'weigh out', 'stock-in-trade'.

The quality the poet most values in story-telling is the random, or unplanned element. There is an effective image used to convey this part of the story-telling process:

> Assemble, first, all casual bits and scraps
> That may shake down into a world perhaps.

The 'casual bits and scraps' and the word 'may' convey this random element, yet the most telling touches are 'perhaps' (which is further emphasized by the rhyme) and the use of 'shake down', a verb which perfectly captures the vague, unpredictable aspect of the process the poet is trying to communicate. These associations are developed in the following lines with 'by chance' and 'random'. The proper material of 'story-telling', ordinary people whom we do not know and about whom we are therefore free to imagine what we like ('guessed idly at') are typified in an image which recalls the sort of activities outlined in Poem B:

> The teashop sort, or travelers in a train
> Seen once, guessed idly at, not seen again.

Such a process may seem maddeningly imprecise and vague, with the writer free to do as he chooses (and perhaps not always sure what he is doing) and creating purely from his imagination. Yet the writer is proposing a form of fiction directly opposed to excessive realism and the sort of literature that provides an instantly recognizable 'slice of life', 'kitchen sink' type situation. The poet says the 'story-teller' must also avoid all temptation to moralize or draw conclusions. This is emphasized in an image rich in 'tongue-in-cheek' irony:

> Sigh then, or frown, but leave (as in despair)
> Motive and end and moral in the air.

D.H. Lawrence felt that if you try to 'nail anything down in the novel' — i.e. if the writer tries to define things too clearly — you will either 'kill' the novel or it will 'get up and walk off with the nail'. Either way the writer loses — either by being too heavily didactic or by losing the control he seeks too earnestly. The poet here is stating a similar view. If his advice is followed, the 'devil' ironically concludes, his seemingly chaotic approach will not only delight with unexpected 'surprise', it will also read more 'human and exact'.

Poem D   Poetry frequently derives strength from the use of contrast, as we have already seen, especially in the previous poems. In Poem D, a constrast is presented between the achievement of Shakespeare and that of other writers. This is immediately established in the balance of the pointed statements that open the poem in an arresting manner. 'Others abide our question' suggests that the 'ordinary' writer remains with us and amongst us, or perhaps we may take 'abide' in the sense of 'submit' to our 'question'; as such, he is limited by common mortality and fails to transcend the doubts and weaknesses that afflict us all. Shakespeare, however, is introduced in a statement of striking simplicity: 'Thou art free'. This use of contrast is repeated in the following lines, where 'we ask and ask', yet Shakespeare 'smiles' and is 'still' — an image of serenity and wisdom, in which Shakespeare is seen as 'Out-topping knowledge'. This is a common poetic device — and one, appropriately enough, for which Shakespeare was particularly famous — where a poet forms a new word, such as 'out-topping', to achieve a more intense or concentrated effect, rather than using a more protracted or rambling phrase to convey the same meaning.

There then follows a metaphor, in which Shakespeare is implicitly compared to the 'loftiest hill'. Because this metaphor is sustained over six lines, we may call it an *extended metaphor*. (If a simile is extended over a series of lines, it is known as an *epic simile*.) 'Loftiest' suggests height and airiness that 'tall' or 'high' would not convey — though it is interesting that the poet uses 'hill' rather than the more grand 'mountain'. Still, 'hill' is sufficiently high for its peak or 'crown' to be visible only to the 'stars' and sky. The Shakespearean achievement is seen exclusively in hyperbolic terms of peaks and pinnacles — 'out-topping', 'loftiest', 'majesty', 'Heaven of heavens', 'stars and sunbeams', 'victorious brow'. The advantage of using an extended metaphor means that specific qualities can be highlighted in the elaborated comparison. 'Planting his steadfast footsteps in the sea' has a firm, purposeful ring, suggested by the words 'planting' and 'steadfast' and accentuated by the full, heavy vowel sounds which arrest the rhythm. The implied comparison between Shakespeare and the 'loftiest hill' is emphasized by the use of personification, as the pronoun 'his' becomes deliberately ambiguous, equally applicable to both Shakespeare and the hill. The repetition of the smooth *s* sound here also aids the flowing firmness of this image. The true 'dwelling place' for the peak of the hill contrasts with that of the base, as it is the 'Heaven of heavens' — the most emphatic use of hyperbole in the poem. As the metaphor closes, the contrast is complete:

> Spares but the cloudy border of his base
> To the foiled searching of mortality.

There is almost a hint of condescension in 'spares', while 'cloudy border of his base' suggests that we struggle to comprehend even the lowest point of such genius. The short-comings of our limited understanding are further highlighted in 'the foiled searching of mortality'.

The opening of the sestet directly addresses Shakespeare. There is a formal, elevated sense of 'proclamation' behind 'who didst the stars and sunbeams know' and an alliteration on the flowing smoothness of the *s* sound which culminates in the triumphant praise of:

> Self-schooled, self-scanned, self-honored, self-secure.

Again we have the concentrated impact that can come from compressing a host of associations and implications in newly coined words. In many ways this resounding line stands as a climax to the poem's tribute to Shakespeare, whose achievement is thus seen as unique, orginal and 'self-styled'. 'Didst tread on earth unguessed at' once more suggests the disparity between Shakespeare's genius and our struggle to comprehend it. 'Tread' manages to suggest firmness and the leaving of a clear mark, without implying a plodding sense of 'dragging one's feet', while 'earth' reminds us of *our* rooted and limited status.

In the final three lines, the Shakespearean achievement is related in purely human terms, without any abstract metaphors. Shakespeare is seen as having given consummate expression to the pain and weakness and dilemmas that the 'immortal spirit' must endure. Although Shakespeare has been presented as a being apart from the rest of us, we are now 're-united' as fellow humans, all of us possessing this 'immortal spirit'. Yet his superlative achievement remains and after the heavy, 'oppressive' nature of 'endure', 'impairs' and 'bow', there is a sense of triumph in the final image that celebrates Shakespeare's portrayals of the human situation:

> Find their sole speech in that victorious brow.

There is a curious, perhaps unsatisfactory, quality about this final, mixed metaphor. 'Sole speech' reminds us of Shakespeare's unique achievement ('sole') and also of his humanity ('speech') after metaphors of lofty hills. Yet one would expect to find speech, sole or otherwise, in the mouth, or on the lips. 'Victorious brow' certainly recalls the images of peaks and pinnacles, the brow being the topmost part of the face (or, appropriately, hill). Perhaps the poet is suggesting that the history of the struggles and doubts and weaknesses of our human situation is written on the 'brow' of Shakespeare himself, in the sense of 'weathered brow'. The main point is that such a poem should surely reach a note of pronounced assertion at the end — yet this statement appears a little vague and perhaps a little flat. As a climax, it seems to lack the clarity and impact which the poem has already achieved (perhaps too early) in:

> Self-schooled, self-scanned, self-honored, self-secure,
> Didst tread on earth unguessed at.

The most satisfying aspect of the conclusion lies in the finality of the closing rhyme, where there is a pronounced and emphatic repetition of sound in 'bow' and 'brow'.

Poem E　　We have so far seen how imagery can be used to create atmosphere or to illustrate and develop an idea. Poem E employs imagery in the more traditional manner of enhancing the beauty and vitality of a series of sensuous, natural descriptions. Indeed, when it comes to such poetry, our example here is one of the finest. The imagery of the opening stanza suggests a feeling of fullness and fruition, through such words as 'mellow', 'maturing', 'ripeness' and 'oe'rbrimmed'. The opening line has a gentle smoothness that is helped by the alliteration of 'mists and mellow'. This *m* sound threads softly and consistently through the entire poem, as if to suggest the gentle background hum of bees and other insects on a warm summer's day. Both the season of autumn and the 'maturing' sun are personified (all aspects of Nature here are 'teeming' with life) as 'bosom' friends (which suggests a particularly intimate closeness) — who 'conspire' together to bring fruition to everything. 'Conspire' may seem an odd choice, yet here it carries nothing of the secret menace usually associated with the word. Perhaps the poet has the Latin derivation of the word in mind, which means to 'breathe together' — a meaning that is more suited to the present purpose here. The richness of atmosphere in this opening stanza comes largely from the use of verbs — 'to load and bless/With fruit', 'To bend with apples the mossed cottage-trees' (a particularly effective visual image) — and alliteration such as 'fill all fruit with ripeness to the core', the *f* sound being a protracted, drawn out sound that suggests 'spilling over'. The rounded, heavy vowel sounds are part of the tactile images which suggest a fullness we can almost feel in our hands:

> To swell the gourd and plump the hazel-shells.

'Swell', 'gourd', and 'plump' are all richly evocative here. The image of the bees that are almost intoxicated by the abundance of warmth, perfume and nectar, typifies the richness of the entire stanza:

> For Summer has oe'rbrimmed their clammy cells.

Here, the 'humming' *m* sound is particularly emphasized. After the visual impact of 'oe'rbrimmed', there follows the marvellous tactile quality of 'clammy'.

There is a slightly different quality to the imagery, and consequently the atmosphere, in the second stanza. The rich abundance of stanza one gives way to the serene, quiet, almost lethargic feeling that comes with too many warm days. The stanza opens with a rhetorical question — i.e. a question whose answer is obvious, or implied in the question itself (here the answer would be 'everyone'). The stanza then unfolds as an elaborate and prolonged continuation of the personification of autumn, 'who' is now seen in a series of 'his' typical settings. The first image suggests peace and calm, with autumn:

> sitting careless on a granary floor,
> Thy hair soft-lifted by the winnowing wind.

This is a striking visual image, with the final, post-harvest scraps of straw (autumn's 'hair') gently 'lifted' by the occasional breeze. The aural effect of the alliteration in 'winnowing wind' suggests the breath of wind itself in the repeated *w* sound. The rhythm here, notably 'soft-lifted', conveys the lifting movement of the straw. The second image suggests weariness and a well-earned rest from harvest toil:

> Or on a half-reaped furrow sound asleep,
>> Drowsed with the fume of poppies, while thy hook
>>> Spares the next swath and all its twined flowers.

The first half of the image uses heavy syllables ('furrow', 'sound'), which produce a soporific effect as the field is left 'half-reaped'. 'Drowsed with the fume of poppies' attempts a difficult image of smell to convey the narcotic, sleep-inducing properties of the poppy. The 'hook', or scythe, remains idle, though there is a reminder of its 'swishing' sound in the alliteration of 'spares the next swath'. The poet also suggests the now slightly neglected abundant excess, even disorder, in the image of the 'twined flowers', which have so grown and proliferated that they tangle — a tangle which the weary labourer no longer has the desire to tidy.

The images continue to build up in separate, self-contained pictures. The next image suggests great stillness, with autumn, in the form of a heavily laden tree, 'bending' over a brook like a gleaner — the person who follows the harvesters, bending to collect the corn the reapers may have missed (an exclusively autumnal occupation). Once again, it is the final image that best typifies the stanza's predominant feeling:

> Or by a cider-press, with patient look,
>> Thou watchest the last oozings hours by hours.

Here the stillness and slight weariness are again captured. The *s* sound is again used, this time to convey the squeezing of the apple-juice. Yet the most effective word here is the richly onomatopoeic 'oozings', which suggests both the movement and the sound of the cider-press, while also conveying a sense of taste that is deliciously full.

Once more there is a shift of feeling into the third stanza. Just as the hint of excess ('clammy') prepares us for the feeling of almost oppressive abundance in the following stanza, so 'last oozings' begins to suggest the sense of autumn ending and the onset of winter, that prevails in the final stanza. The rich details now give way to more sparse, slightly fragmented images, as the fullness of summer moves towards the bleakness of winter. Whereas the imagery in the first two stanzas covers the full range of our senses, in the final stanza it is predominantly aural — which is a less immediate or sensuous form of imagery than the earlier visual and tactile impressions. This is introduced when the poet tells us he will talk now of the 'songs' of autumn, a type of music which still possesses great beauty and is not inferior to the more celebrated 'music' of spring.

The setting is now different:

> While barred clouds bloom the soft-dying day,
> And touch the stubble plains with rosy hue.

Although this is an evocative visual image of the reds and pinks of an autumn sunset, there are other, subtle suggestions here. The very introduction of clouds — even with their 'barred', translucent beauty — and the soft cadence of 'soft-dying day' introduce a new note into the poem. And although the fields are covered with an incandescent 'rosy' hue, they are now 'stubble plains' — cropped and somehow finished with. The first aural image, the buzzing of the 'small gnats' may well be the 'music' of a 'choir', but it is a 'wailful choir' that 'mourns'. A visual impression of their undulating, grouped movement is carried in:

> borne aloft
> Or sinking, as the light wind lives or dies

where the rhythm suggests their motion in the 'run-on' effect of 'borne aloft/Or sinking' and the phrase 'lives or dies'. Their 'music' is captured in the repetition of the *s* consonant. The lambs are now 'full grown' — all the earlier sensations of a landscape 'bursting with life' are now completed — and their 'music', the onomatopoeic 'bleat', is a broken, disconcerting sound. The final images of 'song' complete the poem's subtle movement:

> Hedge crickets sing; and now with treble soft
> The redbreast whistles from a garden croft;
> And gathering swallows twitter in the skies.

The poem has moved from the richness of late summer to the coming of winter. The first two stanzas surround and almost overwhelm us with their abundant suggestions. Now the focus is slowly moved to the 'mournful' greyness of a late autumn sunset. The final 'songs' are pregnant with associations — associations that may not be instinctively apparent to non-native students. The chirping of the hedge crickets is a hard, clipped sound. The redbreast is the traditional bird of winter and he appears to remind us of what is to come. The *f* and *s* sounds delicately convey the redbreast's gentle, yet clear 'music'. The final image holds a certain sadness, as the swallows 'gather' only to migrate. One of the more remarkable triumphs of this poem lies in this final image. After the sensuous and seductive celebration of autumn's ripe maturity that has gone before, the concluding, haunting impression is of the fragmented, almost cacophonous, onomatopoeic 'twitter' of the departing swallows.

CONCLUSION

Apart from attempting to look at imagery 'in action' through our specific examples of the reference poems, this summary of the potential and nature of imagery is necessarily general for one obvious reason. When a poet writes a poem, he seeks to invest his treatment of his theme — a theme that may often be conventional and 'well-worn' — with fresh insight. The key to his success here will lie in his use of imagery. Consequently he will search for a sense of freshness, or surprise, in his images which will be sharply, illuminatingly and, perhaps, unexpectedly different from previous poems. In a real sense, each poem attempts to be unique in its use of imagery; and the most effective poetry will succeed in this. Anything other than generalizations which alert the student to the possibilities and function of imagery would be misleading and ultimately meaningless. As ever, the student will have to draw on his background knowledge and experience for guidance and direction, yet he must focus his attention as sensitively and as relevantly as possible on the specific poem he has before him. This new poem will require an immediate and personal response which the student cannot 'rehearse' or become 'word-perfect' in, formula fashion, before he becomes acquainted with the actual poem in question.

EXERCISES

1. Bent double, like old beggars under sacks,
   Knock-kneed, coughing like hags, we cursed through sludge,
   Till on the haunting flares we turned our backs,
   And towards our distant rest began to trudge.
   Men marched asleep. Many had lost their boots,
   But limped on, blood-shod. All went lame, all blind;
   Drunk with fatigue; deaf even to the hoots
   Of gas-shells dropping softly behind.

   a. Comment on the visual, aural and tactile images used here to convey the feeling of weary soldiers leaving the battle-front.
   b. Which images strike you as the most effective?

2. In Xanadou did Kubla Khan
   A stately pleasure dome decree:
   Where Alph, the sacred river, ran
   Through caverns measureless to man
       Down to a sunless sea.
   So twice five miles of fertile ground
   With walls and towers were girdled round:
   And there were gardens bright with sinuous rills,
   Where blossomed many an incense-bearing tree;
   And here were forests ancient as the hills,
   Enfolding sunny spots of greenery.

a. This poem depends heavily on the creation of an exotic, mysterious atmosphere. How does the imagery contribute to such an atmosphere in this opening stanza?

3. He disappeared in the dead of winter:
   The brooks were frozen, the airports almost deserted,
   And snow disfigured the public statues;
   The mercury sank in the mouth of the dying day.
   O all the instruments agree
   The day of his death was a dark cold day.

a. This poem commemorates the death of the poet W.B. Yeats. How is imagery used to suggest how the poet feels towards Yeats?

4. Left to herself, the serpent now began
   To change; her elfin blood in madness ran,
   Her mouth foamed, and the grass, therewith besprent,
   Withered at dew so sweet and virulent;
   Her eyes in torture fixed, and anguish drear,
   Hot, glazed, and wide, with lid lashes all sear,
   Flashed phosphor and sharp sparks, without one cooling tear.
   The colours all inflamed throughout her train,
   She writhed about, convulsed with scarlet pain:
   A deep volcanian yellow took the place
   Of her milder-mooned body's grace;
   And, as the lava ravishes the mead,
   Spoilt all her silver mail, and golden brede.

a. This passage deals with the magical transformation of a snake into a beautiful woman. Comment on the imagery used in the description, especially its visual quality.
b. Comment on 'scarlet pain' and 'volcanian yellow'.

5.   The flower
          fallen
     she saw it
          where
     it lay
          a pink petal

     intact
          deftly
     placed it

          on
     its stem
          again

a.   This may be called an 'imagist' poem, where a single image is
     simply presented without further development or comment. The
     image itself is intended to work directly upon the reader to arouse
     certain feelings, emotions etc. What is the effect of the image
     presented here?

6.   There were never strawberries
     like the ones we had
     that sultry afternoon
     sitting on the step
     of the open french window
     facing each other
     your knees held in mine
     the blue plates in our laps
     the strawberries glistening
     in the hot sunlight
     we dipped them in sugar
     looking at each other.

a.   How is imagery used in this description to comment on the quality
     of the memory of a past relationship?

CHAPTER 8

R H Y T H M

RHYTHM AND METRE

Before looking in detail at rhythm, we will have to comment briefly on the question of metre, as the two often confuse students. It would be better if we could ignore the issue of metre completely — Advanced Level examining boards no longer desire any detailed understanding of its intricacies. Yet there are two reasons, perhaps, why we cannot. Firstly it is a concept that students studying poetry will inevitably come across and therefore it requires some sort of clarification; 'Oh, don't trouble yourselves with that' is hardly satisfactory. Also, many students are 'seduced' by the mechanical nature of metre. Here, at last in poetry appreciation, appears something quantifiable and concrete, something that can be learnt, formula-fashion, and re-gurgitated faultlessly in the examination room. I have read many scripts by students that have made triumphant, yet meaningless, proclamations about spondaics and dactylics. As such observations (even when correct) say little of importance about the poem in question, and may divert the analysis from more important considerations, some explanation becomes necessary.

The other reason we must consider metre to some extent is that, although metre may seem artificial and irrelevant to us, it was an important consideration for poets writing before modern times. The controlled strength and momentum behind the lines of Shakespeare and Milton and Pope, for instance, owe much to the inherent metrical patterning of blank verse or heroic couplets.

The concept of *metre* arose from principles laid down by following the precepts of Classical Greek and Latin verse at a time when English poetry was, so to speak, just beginning to find its own feet. Such principles state that a line of verse should follow a *precise and regular pattern*, in terms of the number of syllables per line and the arrangement of stressed and unstressed syllables within that line. It was seen as an imperceptible force to keep the poem tightly-knit and unified. *Rhythm*, on the other hand, refers to the way in which the lines are *actually read*. It is the movement of the verse, it is clearly a far more important consideration.

The only form of verse that is actually read according to its fixed pattern — that is, where metre and rhythm are identical — is the nursery rhyme, or doggerel. This can be seen in something like:

> Húmpt̆y Dúmpt̆y sát ŏn á wáll,
> Húmpt̆y Dúmpt̆y hád ă gréat fáll

which is recited without variation throughout. This 'sing-song', simple regularity is particularly appealing to children, who can quickly pick up the movement and join in. With more serious poetry, the rhythm will not necessarily follow the metre and will often emphasize crucial words by departing from the metrical pattern (i.e. when a syllable that, according to the metre should be unstressed, is actually stressed).

One famous example will serve as a final comment on metre. Let us look at the opening line of Sonnet XVIII by Shakespeare:

> Shall I compare thee to a Summer's day?

The metre of the sonnet in English is usually iambic pentameter — the characteristics of which we have already defined in the section on *FORM*. Mechanically reduced to its metrical pattern of five 'feet' of two syllables, containing an unstressed syllable followed by a stressed syllable — and this pattern is by far the most common in English poetry — the line will appear.

> Shăll Í cŏmpáre thĕe tó ă Súmmĕr's dáy?

To read it in this manner would, of course, divest the line of all its impact. The way the line is actually to be read, i.e. its rhythm is:

> Sháll Í cŏmpáre thée tŏ ă Súmmĕr's dáy?

In this way the rhythm emphasizes the two key words — 'thee' and 'Summer's'.

Given such a basic understanding of the origin and purpose of metre, the student today need only pursue the concept and its variations if it particularly interests him. He will find ample material on the subject if he so wishes. It is not to the purpose of this present book to deal with metre, as such, any further.

RHYTHM AND THE REFERENCE POEMS

Poem A The rhythm of a poem, its movement from word to word and from line to line, carries the 'ebb and flow' of the poet's thoughts and emotions. He uses rhythm to emphasize crucial areas of the poem —

often a single word. Rhythm also contributes to a more subtle aspect of poetry, its 'musical' quality — whether smooth and lilting or harsh and dramatic. This can be seen in the opening line of Poem A.

> We are as clouds that veil the midnight moon;

With its airy, gliding lightness this suggests the movement of floating clouds — an impression continued in the next two lines by the use of 'and'. There are two useful guides to rhythm. The first is *word order*. Whenever the poet departs from the normal pattern of English word order, the rhythm will emphasize certain words. Here it is the word 'radiantly' that is "displaced" (we would normally expect it to come before 'Streaking'). In this way the two words that give the image its striking effect — 'Streaking' and 'radiantly' — are deliberately stressed by the rhythm. The second guide is the poet's use of *punctuation*, especially at the end of the lines. There is a different rhythmic effect produced by ending a line with a pause, such as a full-stop, or colon, or semi-colon, than by running one line into the next without any pause. Punctuation within the line — especially question and exclamation marks and dashes — will also have a considerable bearing on the poem's rhythm. In this example at line 3, the exclamation mark further emphasizes the beauty of the image, yet the following dash quickly introduces the next image which negates or defeats this beauty. The colon that closes the first stanza is not as final as a full-stop, as the poet's image of the 'lyre' in stanza two is related to the same idea. However, it still allows for a sufficient pause to enable the implications of stanza one to sink in.

In the second stanza there is a greater flow between the lines, perhaps to suggest the building of a crescendo, as in music (the predominant image). Again, inverted word order is used to highlight a crucial phrase — 'frail frame' — frailty and impermanence being central to the poem's theme. Stanza three brings a series of 'end-stopped' lines — i.e. lines with a punctuated pause at the end, that represent 'self-contained' statements and do not 'run' into the following line. This pattern is continued in the final stanza. The effect is gradually to build up a body of impressions that move firmly and weightily towards a climax — here the poem's final line, where the rhythmic stress falls heavily on the key word 'Mutability'. We also have a slightly disjointed, yet balanced, effect at the opening of stanza three:

> We rest. — A dream has power to poison sleep;
> We rise. — One wandering thought pollutes the day;

Again this is achieved through the use of punctuation. The effect is to emphasize the opening idea — 'resting' and 'rising' — and also, even more tellingly, the following statement that unsettles and negates the first — a pattern we have already noted earlier in the poem. This is repeated (and further emphasized by the exclamation mark) in the opening of the final stanza. Such a device is very much in keeping with the poem's intention of showing how transient joy and beauty are. On the whole, the poem's rhythm is gentle and subtle, in harmony with the quiet assurance of the philosophical tone.

Poem B   Also in keeping with its informal, conversational tone, is the rhythm of Poem B, which has the easy, natural flow of a voice actually speaking to us directly. The physical layout of a poem may also offer a guide to a poet's use of rhythm. Here we can notice how, in each stanza, the poet begins with short opening statements. These short units of verse (in free verse a short line, in other forms of poetry, perhaps a half line that is complete and 'self-contained') will inevitably be stressed and emphasized by the rhythm to arrest the reader's attention. Poem B then follows these opening statements with a series of lines that flow quite freely from one line to the next as the poet accumulates the various details in support of his initial comments. There is constant use of enjambement, as the kaleidoscope of varied, simultaneous, deliberately mundane activities that take place while others are suffering, is built up. The extra length of:

> While someone else is eating or opening a window or just walking dully alone

is particularly effective. The four lines (5–8) move steadily together, regulated by the use of the comma, yet maintaining the momentum. Following this, the shorter:

> They never forgot

is particularly emphasized. This is followed by another series of images — there is only one natural pause, the comma in line 11 — which provides an even stronger sense of gathering movement. Throughout the rhythm is emphasizing key words, especially in lines 10–11, where the enjambement effect highlights 'Anyhow' — a word whose casual, yet inevitable associations are so important to what the poem is trying to communicate. Incidentally, associations of a word such as 'Anyhow' here typify the problem of non-native students perhaps not being totally in tune with such native associations.

The opening of stanza two again suggests the rhythm of the normal speaking voice:

> In Brueghel's Icarus, for instance.

The poet runs the sense of line one into the following line. Such a device usually emphasizes the opening of that following line and here 'Quite leisurely' is heavily stressed. The pattern of opening with short, emphatic statements followed by longer, expanded illustrations is then repeated in the second stanza. As the lines progress, we should notice how the key words are highlighted: 'may', in line 15 (with its vague, perhaps unconcerned associations); 'As it had to', line 18 (carrying its sense of simple inevitability); 'Something amazing', line 20 (with its isolation from the mundane scene that surrounds the 'fall'); and, perhaps most effective of all, 'calmly', in the final line, emphasized by the slightly inverted word order (we would expect 'calmly sailed'), which strongly suggests blissful unawareness of the tragedy.

Free verse does not mean undisciplined verse. In this form of poetry, the poet has to pay particular attention to the rhythmic movement of the lines. Control of rhythm, through line-length and patterning of stanzas, is essential to prevent this type of poetry from becoming loose and meaningless. Consequently the question of rhythm is an especially important one for the student confronting a poem in free verse.

Poem C   The heroic couplet form of Poem C tends to reduce the scope of rhythmic variation, probably more so than all the other forms. Constrained by rhyming in couplets, the lines tend to fall in self-contained, separate units of two lines. This regulates the flow of a poem as a whole, as the pointed effect of the rhyme would be lost in a series of 'run on' lines. Couplets tend to move in a steady, regular rhythm, as the details gradually and weightily accumulate. Balance and control are central to the idea of the heroic couplet form and this is reflected in the ensuing rhythm. Yet if the movement of the lines as a whole is somewhat limited, rhythmic emphasis within the line often becomes more interesting. Here, in the opening lines, the opposition to the poet's views are highlighted by isolating 'some say'. A rare example of enjambement in lines 5–6 again stresses the beliefs the poet is attacking by emphasizing 'Known' — the poet's view being that story-tellers should deal with the fictional, or 'unknown'. In line 8, the rhythmic stress falls on 'conscientiously' — partly through inverted word order and partly because of the complex rhythm inherent in the long word itself, which attracts attention. Again it is a key word, forcefully ironic in making the poet's point. In line 13 the rhythm picks out 'by chance' — again to highlight an important issue in his argument which is the 'random' element in the selection of 'story-telling' material. This is further enhanced by the precision and clear delineation (so suitable for 'advice', or instruction-giving) of:

> Seen once, guessed idly at, not seen again

which pin-points the varied, unexpected and uncertain quality the 'story-teller' must seek. The way in which heroic couplets build up their effect leads us to expect some sort of climax of effect. Here, two of the concluding lines:

> Their own and your own and your readers' eyes,

and

> Motive and end and moral in the air,

use the repetition of 'and' to convey a feeling of gathering momentum as the poem moves towards its emphatic final assertion.

Poem D   The opening of Poem D is more dramatic. It comes with a series of short, separated, heavily emphasized statements — almost like five peels of a bell. The rhythm demands that each pronouncement be read and then assimilated in a lengthy pause. 'Others abide our question' provides a striking opening, which is then counter-balanced by: 'Thou art free'. Both 'Others' and 'Thou' are heavily stressed, and the poem will unfold around the difference between these two elements — i.e. Shakespeare and the rest of us. The effect is reproduced in line two:

> We ask and ask — Thou smilest and art still

'still' here in the sense of 'untroubled', even serene. The 'run on' into line three provides emphasis for 'Out-topping knowledge'. To see the full effect of rhythm here, it is useful to refer once more, briefly, to metre. This poem is a sonnet and the underlying metre for the sonnet is iambic pentameter. As such, the lines would appear:

> Ŏthérs ăbíde oŭr quéstĭon. Thóu aȓt frée.
> Wĕ aśk aňd aśk — Thŏu smílĕst aňd aȓt stíll,
> Oŭt-tóppĭng knówlĕdge.

However, the rhythm for actually reading these lines is:

> Othĕrs ăbíde oúr quéstĭon. Thóu aȓt free.
> Wé aśk aňd aśk — Thóu aȓt stíll,
> Oút-tóppĭng knówlĕdge.

Here we can see how the preponderance of stressed syllables arrests the rhythm, forcing us to take account of each separate statement.

The following lines expound the glories of Shakespeare's achievement. The details build impressively together as the poet reverses his technique and employs a series of lines that flow smoothly and surely almost without pause. (Technically, lines 3–11 constitute a single sentence.) The climax of this sweeping movement lies in the heavy emphasis of:

> Sélf-schóoled, sélf-scánned, sélf-hónoŭred, sélf-sĕcúre.

This slows the movement down to prepare for the final observation of this line of thought in:

> Didst tréad ŏn eárth uňguéssed át.

The next phrase of this line — 'Better so!' — suggests a philosophical afterthought (and a catching of breath!) and is also emphasized, this time because of its brevity. The final three lines once more produce a flowing movement, yet in a more quiet and sedate manner, in clearly defined, regular segments that allow the full force of the concluding couplet to receive its emphasis.

Poem E   There is a calm, gentle rhythm throughout Poem E. The ripening fullness of late summer is captured at the end of the first stanza in:

.... to set budding more,
And still more, later flowers for the bees,
Until they think warm days will never cease
For Summer has oe'rbrimmed their clammy cells.

This sense of fullness is conveyed rhythmically by the heavily stressed
'And still more'. There is a lovely, lilting quality to line 15:

Thy hair soft-lifted by the winnowing wind

where the rhythm of the line — especially in 'soft-lifted' and 'winnowing'
— 're-enacts' the gentle motion of the bits of straw 'lifting' and rising in
the breeze. The rhythm of the second part of the second stanza becomes
slightly slower and heavier, in keeping with the general feeling of post-
harvest lethargy and weariness:

Or on a half-reaped furrow sound asleep,
Drowsed with the fume of poppies ...

Another striking use of rhythm comes in the final stanza, where the undulating, swaying movement of the 'cloud' of gnats is mirrored in the
movement in the lines:

boŕne ălóft
Oŕ sínkĭng, ăs tħe líght wínd líves ŏr díes.

Here the reading voice rises and falls in the balanced cadence of 'borne
aloft/Or sinking' and 'lives or dies'. As the poem moves from the richness of late summer to the oncoming of sparse winter, the rhythm becomes slightly fragmented and less flowing:

Hedge crickets sing; and now with treble soft
The redbreast whistles from a garden croft;
And gathering swallows twitter in the skies.

CONCLUSION

Rhythm is a subtle, yet crucial element of poetry. Perhaps because of its
subtlety, it is a frequently neglected aspect of students' written analysis
on poetry. The difficulties of rhythm are accentuated all the more for
non-native students. The simple fact remains that all students of English
poetry must acquaint themselves widely with the reading of poetry to develop the ability to read with a sensitive ear for its rhythms.

EXERCISES

1.   Now came still Evening on, and Twilight gray
     Had in her sober Liverie all things clad;
     Silence accompanied, for Beast and Bird,
     They to their grassy Couch, these to their Nests
     Were slunk, all but the wakeful Nightingale;
     She all night long her amorous descant sung;
     Silence was pleased; now glowed the Firmament
     With living Sapphires.

a.   Comment on the overall rhythm of this passage.
b.   How does the rhythm contribute to the atmosphere?

2.   And what shoulder, and what art,
     Could twist the sinews of thy heart?
     And when thy heart began to beat,
     What dread hand? and what dread feet?

     What the hammer? what the chain?
     In what furnace was thy brain?
     What the anvil? what dread grasp
     Dare its deadly terrors clasp?

a.   Comment on the rhythm of this famous description of the creation of
     the tiger.
b.   How does the rhythm relate to the descriptions?

3.   ... happy days
     It was indeed for all of us — for me
     It was a time of rapture! Clear and loud
     The village clock tolled six — I wheeled about,
     Proud and exulting like an untired horse
     That cares not for his home. All shod with steel,
     We hissed along the polished ice in games
     Confederate, imitative of the chase
     And woodland pleasures — the resounding horn,
     The pack loud chiming, the hunted hare.
     So through the darkness and the cold we flew,
     And not a voice was idle.

a.   How is the rhythm here appropriate for this description of children
     skating?

4.   Break, break, break,
             On thy cold gray stones, O Sea!
     And I would that my tongue could utter
             The thoughts that arise in me.

a. Comment on the rhythm of this stanza, especially noting the effect of the repetition.

5. I caught this morning morning's minion, king-
   dom of daylight's dauphin, dapple-dawn-drawn Falcon,
   in his riding
   Of the rolling level underneath him steady air, and striding
High there, how he rung upon the rein of a wimpling wing
In his ecstasy!

a. What does the movement of the verse seek to achieve in this description of the windhover bird?

6. There is no port, there is nowhere to go
only the deepening blackness darkening still
blacker upon the soundless, ungurgling flood
darkness at one with darkness, up and down
and sideways utterly dark, so there is no direction any more
and the little ship is there; yet she is gone.

a. Which words are particularly highlighted by the rhythm in this passage? What do these words have in common?
b. What does the movement of the verse suggest here?

CHAPTER 9

R H Y M E

Rhyme is one of the most obviously aural aspects of poetry and contributes much of the muscial quality of verse. It refers to a similarity in the sounds of words or syllables, usually those coming at the end of a line of verse. In certain forms of poetry — heroic couplets, quatrains, sonnets — the patterning of lines that rhyme is fixed and predetermined by the form itself.

TYPES OF RHYME

Although rhyme may appear a straightforward, 'obvious' device, its effects are frequently quite subtle. For the sake of analysis, it is useful to outline different types of rhyme.

Masculine Rhyme

This is when the final syllable of the rhyme is a stressed syllable as in 'dĕfeát/rĕpeát', 'rĕqueśt/iňveśt'. Such rhyming tends to produce a pronounced or emphatic effect, as in Byron's *Don Juan*:

> The Senhor Don Alfonso stood confused;
> Antonia bustled round the ransacked room,
> And turning up her nose, with looks abused
> Her master, and his myrmidons, of whom
> Not one, except the attorney, was amused.

Much of the emphasis that comes from masculine rhyme derives from the fact that is allows the rhyming of one-syllable words (which are always stressed). Such single syllable rhyming tends to have a pointed and telling impact, as in the opening of Auden's poem 'In Memory of W.B. Yeats':

> Earth, receive an honored guest,
> William Yeats is laid to rest.

Feminine Rhyme

This refers to a rhyme in which the final syllable is unstressed as in 'mórrŏw/sórrŏw' 'fíngĕr/língĕr'. Because the final syllable is unstressed, such rhyming tends to produce a 'falling away' effect, as in Hopkins' 'Inversnaid':

> Of a pool so pitchblack, fell-frowning,
> It rounds and rounds Despair to drowning.

Polysyllabic Rhyme

This is when several syllables are part of the rhyme. Such elaborate rhyming will 'call attention' to itself and is often used to comic or humorous effect, as in Byron's 'intellectual/hen-pecked you all' rhyme already quoted. Such rhyming is heavily emphasized as it arrests the rhythm and flow of a poem quite dramatically.

Para-rhyme

This is also known as *half* or *partial* rhyme. As the name suggests, it indicates sounds that almost rhyme. Such rhyming produces a deliberately uncomfortable, disconcerting effect. One poet who made effective use of such rhyming was Wilfred Owen (in poetry that highlights the tragedy of war):

> And by his mile, I knew that sullen hall;
> By his dead smile, I knew we stood in Hell.
> With a thousand pains that vision's face was grained;
> Yet no blood reached there from the upper ground.

Internal Rhyme

This is the use of rhyme within a single line of verse, an effect that adds particular emphasis and also quickens the pace of the rhythm, as in

Coleridge's 'Ancient Mariner':

> The fair breeze blew, the white foam flew,
> The furrow followed free;
> We were the first that ever burst
> Into that silent sea.

Other Rhymes

Students may come across the concept of *visual* or *sight* rhyme. This indicates words or syllables that look the same on the printed page (e.g. 'bough'/'rough'), yet whose actual sounds do not rhyme. I doubt if such rhyming carries any validity or effect. Poetry should be listened to, a fact which negates sight rhyme, although in reading a poem this device may admittedly link such words together.

Another form of rhyme, which again does not constitute 'true' rhyme, but which may be used for a certain effect, is the exact repetition of the same sound in words that carry different meanings; e.g. 'right'/'write', 'sought'/'sort', 'sight'/'site'.

EFFECT OF RHYME

Rhyme achieves several functions in poetry. Firstly, it effects the rhythm of the verse. In the example quoted above from Coleridge, we can see how sharp, repeated, light, one-syllable rhyme can accelerate the movement quite dramatically. We have already noted how the use of couplet rhyme tends to regulate the rhythm in a steady, assured manner, or how the couplet can be used to convey a sense of finality, with its rounded neatness, as in Milton's:

> At last he rose, and twitch'd his mantle blew:
> Tomorrow to fresh Woods, and Pastures new.

As we read a poem, rhyme may act upon us almost subconsciously, providing a flow and satisfying unity that relates poetry to music. It also has the effect of linking together the words being rhymed — words that one may not usually associate together. This can create an unexpected, or surprise element that forces us to think sharply about what the poet is saying, as in Blake's:

> Love seeketh only Self to please,
> To bind another to Its delight,
> Joys in another's loss of ease,
> And builds a Hell in Heaven's despite.

A final general consideration concerning rhyme relates to its purely aural quality; that is, the actual effect of the sound that is being rhymed. Much of the 'music' of the verse will lie in the type of sounds that are repeated by the rhyme. Obviously this can cover a range of effects, from the full rich effect of Hopkins':

> When weeds, in wheels, shoot long and lovely and lush;
> Thrush's eggs look little low heavens, and thrush . . .

to the gentle, lyrical quality of Tennyson's:

> But such a tide as moving seems asleep,
> > Too full for sound and foam,
> When that which drew from out the boundless deep
> > Turns again home.

or the harsh, grating effect of Owen's:

> What passing bells for these who die as cattle?
> Only the monstrous anger of the guns.
> Only the stuttering rifles' rapid rattle
> Can patter out their hasty orisons.

RHYME AND THE REFERENCE POEMS

Poem A   Here the rhyme scheme is constant, in a quatrain pattern of *abab* — a full and complete use of rhyme that brings a steady movement and overall harmony to the poem as a whole. The rhyme is basically light, one-syllable rhyme. It is also full in the sense that the similarities in sound of the rhymed words tend to be exact — 'moon'/'soon', 'sleep'/'weep'. This all contributes to the poem's integrated, tightly-knit structure and also provides a satisfying musical resonance. The rhyming is smooth and flowing, in keeping with the calm, assured tone of the poem. The rhyme here adds particular emphasis to the poem's conclusion.

Poem B   Although we have described this poem as free verse — a form that makes little, if any, use of rhyme — this particular poem employs a subtle, irregular rhyme patterning throughout. As the poet is seeking an effect of colloquial realism — giving the impression of an informal, speaking voice — full and obvious rhyming would be inappropriately formal and obtrusive. Occasionally rhyme is used here for emphasis ('away'/'may', 'green'/'seen') in couplet fashion, yet its main role is to thread quietly through the poem, a device that brings unity and tightness to the overall structure and effect. It is a use of rhyme that draws little attention to itself; indeed it takes several readings before many readers are aware that the poem makes such extensive use of rhyme. The concluding rhyme of 'on' with 'shone' provides just the right note of gentle, fading finality and inevitability as the poem closes.

Poem C   This poem depends heavily on rhyme for its impact. This is inevitable with a form such as heroic couplets, where the rhyme neatly rounds off the point being made. The rhyme is emphatic, one syllable, masculine rhyme throughout:

> To forge a picture that will pass for true,
> Do conscientiously what liars do.

The rhyme lends a sense of balance, control and completion. It is also used to underline the occasional use of irony or humour, conveying strongly the impression of a sophisticated, intelligent mind at work:

> Sigh then or frown, but leave (as in despair)
> Motive and end and moral in the air;

The rhyme is particularly pronounced in the concluding couplet, where the forceful, striking use of the 'act' syllable — and we can feel the 'work' our mouth has to do to produce this sound — suggests just the right feeling of finality, of no further argument:

> Nice contradiction between fact and fact
> Will make the whole read human and exact.

Poem D   This sonnet uses a rhyme scheme of *abba acca* in the octave. The repetition of this *a* rhyme, on the *ee* sound ('free', 'majesty', 'sea', 'mortality') is particularly effective. Firstly it unites the eight lines with its continuity — especially in the consecutive rhyme of lines four and five across a break in the verse. There is also a slight variation in the rhyme; all are full rhymes, yet 'majesty' and 'mortality', also linked by the *m* sound, extend the *ee* rhyme to 'tee'. Furthermore, there is a pleasing, light, open quality to the *ee* rhyme which adds a certain music to the elaborate praise.

As the poet develops his thought more seriously in the sestet, the rhymes become heavier and more pronounced, slowing the rhythm and emphasizing the point being made ('know'/'so', 'secure'/'endure'). This is especially seen in the poem's concluding couplet. Here, 'bow' and 'brow' are almost exact repetition and the weight of the poem's conclusion is carried by the heavy *ow* rhyme and the accentuated repetition of the strong *b* consonant.

Poem E   Rhyme schemes in odes tend to be elaborate. Here it follows a pattern of *ababcdedcce*. Such patterning creates a fluid, interweaving harmony and movement. The sense of fullness in stanza one is mirrored in the fullness of the one-syllable rhymes. Apart from the 'ness'/'bless' rhyme, all the rhymes in this stanza are 'voiced' — a term that indicates a sound that is produced by vibrating the vocal chords. Such sounds are richer and fuller than 'voiceless' sounds. (We can see the difference in the sounds at the beginning of 'sip' and 'zip'. If one says the two sounds one after another, repeatedly, while touching the 'Adam's apple' of the neck, one can feel this movement and 'voicing' of the vocal chords.) The 'trees'/'bees' rhyme has a richly onomatopoeic, humming quality, which is also echoed in the *z* sound of 'shells'/'bells'.

The slight impression of weariness in stanza two is also helped by the use of rhyme. This can be sensed in the long vowel rhyme of 'store'/'floor' and the more elaborate, falling feminine rhyme of 'flowers'/'hours'. The atmosphere and tone of the final stanza are also captured by the rhyme. There is a sad, heavy quality to 'mourn'/'bourn'. The rhyme of 'aloft'/'soft'/'croft' is far less rich or resonant than the rhyming in the earlier parts of the poem and the poem fades on the soft, gentle rhyme of 'dies'/'skies'.

EXERCISES

1. Thither no more the peasant shall repair
    To sweet oblivion of his daily care;
    No more the farmer's news, the barber's tale,
    No more the wood-man's ballad shall prevail;
    No more the smith his dusky brow shall clear,
    Relax his ponderous strength, and lean to hear;
    The host himself no longer shall be found
    Careful to see the mantling bliss go round;
    Nor the coy maid, half willing to be pressed,
    Shall kiss the cup to pass it to the rest.

    a. How does rhyme affect the rhythm of this passage?
    b. How does rhyme contribute to the atmosphere of the deserted village?

2. She walks in beauty, like the night
          Of cloudless climes and starry skies:
    And all that's best of dark and bright
          Meet in her aspect and her eyes:
    Thus mellowed to that tender light
          Which heaven to gaudy day denies.

    a. How does rhyme add to the movement of the verse here?
    b. How does rhyme contribute to the 'music' of the description?

3. G-r-r-r — there go, my heart's abhorrence!
          Water your damned flowerpots, do!
    If hate killed men, Brother Lawrence,
          God's blood, would not mine kill you!
    What? your myrtle bush wants trimming?

> Oh, that rose has prior claims —
> Needs its leaden vase filled brimming?
> Hell dry you up with its flames!

a. How is rhyme used to emphasize the effect of this comically venomous passage?

4. Where the quiet-colored end of evening smiles,
> Miles and miles
> On the solitary pastures where our sheep
> Half asleep
> Tinkle homeward through the twilight, stray or stop
> As they crop —
> Was the site once of a city great and gay
> (So they say),
> Of our country's very capital, its prince
> Ages since
> Held his court in, gathered councils, wielding far
> Peace or war.

a. Comment on the rhythmic and aural effects of this unusual use of rhyme.

5. His mind is concrete and fastidious,
> His nose is remarkably big;
> His visage is more or less hideous,
> His beard it resembles a wig.

> He has ears, and two eyes, and ten fingers,
> Leastways if you reckon two thumbs;
> Long ago he was one of the singers,
> But now he is one of the dumbs.

a. How does rhyme add to the comic effect of these lines?

6. Thus I
Pass by,
And die:
As One
Unknown,
And gone:
I'm made
A shade,
And laid
I'th'grave,
There have
My cave.
Where tell

I dwell,
FAREWELL.

a. What is the poet trying to achieve here through such a use of rhyme?
Is it effective?

7. A man so various, that he seemed to be
Not one, but all mankind's epitome:
Stiff in opinions, always in the wrong;
Was everything by starts, and nothing long;
But, in the course of one revolving moon,
Was chemist, fiddler, statesman, and buffoon.

a. Comment on the use of rhyme here.

CHAPTER 10

INTENTION

WHAT IS MEANT BY INTENTION

Having spent a considerable amount of time reading the poem, assessing its theme and analysing its details and elements, we should then be in a position to comment on the poet's *intention*. Previous analysis will have concentrated on *how* the poem is written and presented, but in considering intention we will have to ask the more fundamental question of *why* it was written. What is it the poet is trying to achieve, or communicate? What has moved him, or troubled him, to the extent of his undertaking the elaborate, demanding task of creating a poem that will convey, as closely and as effectively as possible, what he really has to say? And demanding the task is. All students of poetry should be encouraged to make their own attempts at writing poetry, if only for the insight the experience will offer into how difficult and frustrating the process can be.W.B.Yeats, who wrote extensively throughout his long life and who was far from being a lazy writer, felt that if, at the end of a day's writing, he had produced about five lines of verse with which he was reasonably satisfied (but which he might possibly change or reject later), then it would have been a day of considerable toil and effort.

We will begin to acquire a clearer view of the poet's intention the longer we 'live' with a poem. This is why the student should not attempt any profoundly penetrating observations too early in his analysis. It is only by working through the details of the poem (form, rhythm, rhyme, imagery etc.) that an increasing and relevant awareness of the overall intention will develop. As he does this, fresh revelations about certain aspects of the poem may force him to modify his earlier impressions, or perhaps confirm them more fully. The need, as ever, is for a flexible, open concentration on such details as they stand before him.

INTENTION AND THE REFERENCE POEMS

By taking the reference poems in isolated segments (form, rhythm, imagery etc.), we have attempted to highlight the specific nature of the various elements of poetry appreciation. Yet all these aspects are inextricably linked and move to achieve the overall intention. Looking at details in isolation has been useful for the present purpose, although in terms of practical poetry analysis, it is somewhat artificial. Observations and suggestions about intention can often be fruitfully made, in passing as it were, as one looks at some of the elements of the poem, particularly imagery. These observations may then be gathered and summarized at the end of the analysis. To look at intention now, in isolation, is perhaps even more artificial than to do so with form, rhythm etc., as *what* a poem has to say is so vitally connected with the *way* in which it is said. Bearing this in mind, however, we may usefully complete the exercise of the reference poems by looking at the intention behind them.

Poem A   This poem attempts to remind us of the central fact of our human existence: that nothing remains unchanged, in its original state, forever. This is offered as a philosophical observation, rather than in a preaching, or didactic, manner. Images of beauty and harmony are presented and shown to be transient and evanescent. Used as similes, they are held to be typical of human life as a whole. This belief that 'all things must pass' is not presented in a pessimistic or gloomy way — the poem is too light and delicate in touch and tone for that. For if there is a certain sadness in the fact that beauty and joy do not last, then there is also a sense of relief and comfort in the fact that neither do grief and sorrow:

> For be it joy or sorrow,
> The path of its departure still is free.

In the end, the poem simply states the one law of Nature which there is no contradicting, in which, paradoxically the only thing that does not change is change itself:

> Nought may endure but Mutability.

Poem B   The contention of this poem is that, for all our professed concern for our follow man, in moments of intensity or crisis we are each of us alone, separate and isolated, in our personal catastrophe. Whether this is because we are basically indifferent and uncaring, or whether it is because such moments cannot possibly be shared anyway, is, perhaps, left open. The fact that the horse is exonerated as being 'innocent' (the rest of us, by implication, being 'guilty') and the use of terms such as 'Quite leisurely', 'may have heard the splash', 'for him it was not an important failure', 'must have seen/Something amazing' and 'sailed calmly on' all suggest a certain criticism. However, there is also a strong sense of inevitability in the poem, that nothing can be done to change things, in the use of statements such as 'must run its course/Anyhow' and 'the sun shone/As it had to'. Perhaps the poet is merely describing 'the way things are' without concerning himself with assigning blame. Frequently, literature is most effective when it contents itself with presenting issues rather than attempting glib, or simplistic solutions. As such, the reader is left to ponder the implications for himself.

Poem C   Of the five reference poems. this is the one that has the most 'designs' on us; that is, it seeks to change or influence the way we think. (Some might say, for this same reason, that it is the least poetic of the five.) The poet presents his views on what constitutes true fiction ('story-telling'). Although the poem proceeds with a certain 'tongue-in-cheek' irony and humour — typified by the title — there is a serious desire here to correct misguided notions about the writing of fiction. The poet feels that the widespread belief that such writing should be realistic and 'true to life' is the wrong approach. The writer, says the poet, must seek to create imaginatively and not slavishly try to imitate or mirror life. In this context of the poem's intention, the use of the word 'forge' is particularly loaded. It is used for ironic effect in the sense of forgery, but it also has connotations of tough, firm creative craftsmanship in the sense of blacksmith's forge. The 'random' element, which need not mean undisciplined or careless writing, is seen as crucial. The writer will stifle his creation if he seeks too much rigid control and 'probability'. In a sense, the story will evolve a life of its own, which the writer must follow. This will not only bring an element of surprise and variety to delight the reader — and the poet is aware that literature must, in some sense, entertain — but ironically it will also, in the end, make the writing more life-like, or, as he states, 'human and exact'. (There is an interesting analogy here with the 'special effects' sounds used on tape and radio. The noise required — a horse's hoofbeat, breaking glass etc — has to be produced 'artificially', as a recording of the actual sound itself, ironically, does not achieve a realistic effect.) Complex, abstract literary theory may not seem particularly appealing as a theme for poetry, yet the ironic stance adopted by the poet in his presentation makes the piece both amusing and interesting.

Poem D   The intention here is not simply to pay homage to the achievement of Shakespeare. It is also an attempt to assess the way we relate to that achievement and define the value it holds for us. The poet feels it is difficult for us to comprehend the nature of Shakespeare's genius, so vast is the chasm that separates us. What remains, however, is the satisfaction and comfort that many of man's most intense experiences, perhaps the sort the poet in Poem B had in mind, find consummate expression in Shakespeare's work. If we despair, either as inadequate writers or suffering human beings, that this 'loftiest hill' is so far above us, in the end it is 'better so' that one man was able to leave such a literary and philosophical legacy.

Poem E   In a 'pure' and traditional sense, this poem is the most poetic of the five, as it seeks to give the reader a sensuous impression of the feeling and spirit of autumn. Its scope extends across a varied range of Nature's autumnal aspects. It celebrates the beauty of the season and seeks to involve the reader in that beauty as vividly as possible. There is a subtle movement through the stanzas which suggests the progress from morning, to afternoon and then evening and also through the season itself, from late summer, to harvest time, to early winter. It is a poem 'oozing' with matured life and vitality, yet also one of calm serenity. If there is a suggestion in the final stanza that such glories must fade, there is no deep sense of mourning or regret. The unforgettable early images are so vividly conveyed that they remain in the mind as a reminder that the cycle will come round once again. The poem is a particularly fine example of the evocative power of imagery as it is not necessary to have experienced such impressions at first hand to appreciate the beauty of this poem. The sensuous richness of the images, the subtle control of rhythm and gentle music of the verse convey us into the very heart of the autumn landscape that the poet describes.

CHAPTER 11

THE WRITTEN ANALYSIS

GENERAL CONSIDERATIONS

The instructions in the Advanced Level syllabus relating to poetry appreciation in the English Literature examinations state that this paper will provide:

> a single passage for comment or more than one passage for comment and comparison... . The intention of the questions is to test the candidate's ability to read literature critically; he will be required to roganize his response to unseen passages and to present that response as clearly and directly as possible. The questions will be of a kind to allow the candidate's sensibility full play, and will not limit themselves merely to comprehension or paraphrase... . Neither prose nor poetry pre-1550 will be set.
> (Cambridge, 1982)

We have already looked at length at the need for *response* and the importance of developing one's *sensibility* (i.e. the ability to relate sensitively and perceptively to literature) in the section on APPROACH. Once the correct 'approach' has been acquired and the 'critical' faculties developed by a thorough assimilation of the 'elements' of poetry appreciation which we have been examining, we come to the actual written analysis on which the student will be assessed.

The key words, in this respect, from the rubric outlined above, are *organization* and *presentation*. These two factors are crucial aspects of any formal, academic essay, yet they are especially relevant to Advanced Level English, where the student's ability to express himself, as well as the quality of what he has to say, is an important consideration.

ORGANIZATION

It is all too easy for poetry appreciation analysis to become a series of random, disjointed observations, especially when pressured by the examination situation. Such observations may prove stimulating in the context of 'discussion', yet the written analysis must present a structured, integrated essay that moves logically, relevantly and fluently from sentence to sentence and from paragraph to paragraph.

If the student approaches the reading of the poem, or poems, in the manner suggested, he will have a series of notes, underlined words etc. These will then have to be gathered and organized before the student can even think of launching his analysis. A logical frame-work for his observations will be created if he groups them under the following sections.

1. What is the poem about?
   This would involve an introductory statement about the poem's theme, or subject-matter, as we analysed in the section on *SUBJECT*.
2. How is the theme/subject presented?
   This will involve an examination of the poem's elements and the effects they achieve within the poem. A structured ordering of the poetic elements would follow the sequence in which we have looked at them i.e. *form*, followed by *tone*, then, *imagery*, *rhythm* and, if there is any, *rhyme*.
3. What is the poet's overall intention or purpose?
   This will look at what the poet is really trying to achieve or communicate in the poem, as outlined in the section on *INTEN-TION*.
4. How successful is the poem in achieving its purpose?
   Here the student must call on his discrimination to assess just how effective the poem is. This section of the analysis requires evidence that the student has responded to the poem in some way, as he will have to state whether or not he has found the poem effective. He should also give reasons for liking or disliking the poem, reasons that should guard against being over subjective or irrelevant (e.g. 'I dislike this poem because I do not agree with the poet's viewpoint', or 'I like this poem because I like anything to do with trains'). If the student expresses an opinion against the poem, which he is perfectly free to do, he might still consider if there is anything in it that might appeal to others.

The crucial point is obviously section No. 3. It will be the student's reading of the poem's intention that will direct his entire analysis. However, the bulk of marks allocated will relate to section No. 2, the examination of the poetic elements. In dealing with this section, the student has two possible methods of approach. He may either take the poem line by line, pointing out whatever is of interest or importance, be it tone, rhythm, imagery, or rhyme, or he can look at the poem element by element, by saying all he has to say about tone and then rhythm, imagery and so on.

PRESENTATION

How well a student writes, his own 'style', will depend on several factors, ranging from guidance from teachers, to how 'well-read' the student is, to 'instinctive flair' for writing. A mature, distinctive style is not achieved overnight. It evolves over years of practice. Reading widely amongst the critics may help acquaint the student with the 'flavour' of literary criticism, though some students 'adopt' such styles, which can leave their analyses stilted, artificial and littered with such imperatives as '*note the use of...*' etc.

Perhaps the only useful observations that can be offered here concern the layout of the written analysis, especially with regard to the use of quotations. These should be used whenever possible and appropriate to illustrate the point being made. They provide specific pieces of evidence that will keep the analysis direct (as the instructions require), relevant and free from vague generalizations. A simple rule is to quote single words or phrases, in inverted commas, within one's own sentences — e.g. "the use of 'sailed calmly on' highlights this unawareness". If the quotation represents a full line of verse or more, the student should use a colon and set the quotation apart on a separate, indented line — e.g. "the poem's opening lines:

> I am poor brother Lippo, by your leave!
> You need not clap your torches to my face,

are dramatic and arresting".

Students should avoid quoting large sections of the poem, i.e. more than two or three lines. If a general observation is to be made about a series of lines, then the line references should be given. A further point about the use of quotations is that, when using a quotation as part of his own sentence, the student must remember the grammatical flow and construction of that sentence; the quotation becomes part of that sentence and must 'agree' with its grammatical organization. In other words, such statements as: "the poet criticizes the sort of writer who 'raid/The mouths of others'" — where there is a singular/plural disagreement between subject and verb (i.e. writer and raid) — must be avoided. The final point concerning quotations is an obvious one, yet one that is not always heeded: the student must ensure that he quotes accurately and exactly. Indeed the student must ensure he allows time for checking his entire analysis. Errors in spelling, grammar etc. are penalized — and heavily so if they are widespread.

COMPARING POEMS

If two poems are offered for comparison they will inevitably be related in some way. The most obvious 'linking' of the two poems will be a similar subject or theme — e.g. the death of a child, description of a city, etc. However, poems may also be compared in relation to the use they make of the same form (e.g. two sonnets), or they may be two poems with a similar intention (e.g. persuasive poems that attempt to influence our thinking and feeling). Again the student will have to bring method and structure to his analysis.

The opening of the student's comparison should seek to establish what the two poems share in common (e.g. the same form, subject, or intention). The body of the analysis can then concentrate on the *different* means and elements the poems employ to achieve their effect. If the question outlines specific areas for comparison — e.g. use of rhythm, rhyme, imagery etc. — the student can analyse these elements as they are given. If the question requires a general comparison, he can then follow the structure already suggested under the section *ORGANIZATION*.

The student will have two alternative methods of approach when it comes to comparing poems. Firstly, he can take the poems separately. In this way he can undertake a straightforward analysis of the first poem, moving through its elements as suggested. This will be followed by a similar analysis of the second poem, yet here the student will also be required to make points of comparison that will refer back to what has been said about the first poem. In this way, his analysis of the second poem will contain such phrases as — 'unlike the first poem, where the poet ...' and 'as in poem one'. The second analysis must constantly bear in mind what has been said in the first and relate to it.

The other method of approach is to take both poems together and look at the use they make of imagery, rhythm etc. simultaneously. In other words, after the opening remarks that establish the common ground in the two poems, the analysis will proceed from element to element — form, tone, rhythm, imagery, rhyme or the elements specifically requested in the question — and look at the use both poems make of that element. This approach provides a more direct form of comparison, but is, perhaps, the more difficult to organize successfully. Both these methods are equally acceptable and the student is free to choose the one that best suits him.

Having compared the poems in terms of their use of poetic elements, some form of conclusion is essential. Here the student should highlight the main points of similarity and difference. He may then state an opinion as to which poem achieves its purpose more successfully.

FINAL WORDS OF WARNING

Before actually beginning the written analysis, the student would be wise to consider the following factors which frequently, and harmfully, mislead students' readings of a poem.

Archaic language

This refers to a use of language that is no longer common. Students often make comments such as 'archaic' or 'old-fashioned' about the language of poetry written before the twentieth century. However, in its own time, the language would *not* have been archaic, a term which means the *deliberate* use of words no longer in contemporary use. The student should avoid such rash observations if the language of a poem is uniform and consistent. If a particular word or phrase clearly stands out as different from the rest in this respect — such as a modern poem suddenly using 'thee' — it may rightly be described as archaic.

Irregular punctuation

Here I am thinking mainly about poets' use of capital letters. Many students assume that if any poet uses a capital letter for a word, he is investing that word with special significance. However, punctuation in English was not properly systematized and regulated until the nineteenth century. Before this, punctuation such as the use of capitals, was largely a matter of personal choice and preference. Poetry of the seventeenth and eighteenth centuries abounds in such irregular and personalised use of capital letters, as in Pope's:

> What future bliss, he gives not thee to know,
> But gives that Hope to be thy blessing now.
> Hope springs eternal in the human breast:
> Man never Is, but always To be blest.

Once again, the student must be alert to the occasional, rather than regular, use of capitals that may well indicate a particularly significant word — as with 'Mutability', in the last line of reference poem A. Variations in the spellings of words were also equally widespread until the nineteenth century.

Layout

Although the poem in question may be written in a standard form (sonnet, quatrains, etc.), students sometimes miss the form of a poem — and the necessary relevant observations on how form contributes to the poem's effect — when the poet chooses to present the form in a manner that may not be immediately obvious. In other words, the layout of the form may use breaks in the verse where one would not normally associate them in such a form — as in reference poem D which, on the surface, does not look like the sonnet it is; or the poet may omit traditional breaks in the form he is using, as we have seen in Gray's 'Elegy', where the poet writes in quatrains without dividing the verse into separate stanzas. Such devices do not alter the basic form, although the reason behind such variations may offer illuminating insights into the poet's purpose. Poets may also choose to indent certain lines in their presentation of their poem.

Use of Irony

The final word of caution relates directly to what is being said, rather than the physical characteristics of the poem. This concerns the possible use of irony. Before finally committing his observations to writing, the student should ask himself if the poet really means what he appears to be saying. Is the poet being open, or does he say one thing, yet mean another? Does he adopt a position, pretending to feel one thing, yet actually feel something else, — perhaps the opposite? Is he, in other words, being ironic? Students sometimes take a poem too literally and dismiss a poem as extreme or naive, when in fact the poem is rich in subtle irony that involves deeper implications the student may miss completely. The poet is not 'being clever', or 'playing games' with his reader on such occasions. His intention may not be best served by direct statement. Poetry frequently deals with emotions and areas of life that cannot be clearly, or simplistically defined. Because of this, irony and ambiguity (where more than one meaning is possible) are essential if the poet is to treat his theme honestly or effectively.

The key to irony will lie in the poet's *tone*. If the student acquires a sensitive grasp of a poem's tone, he is unlikely to miss any intended irony within the poem. This will limit the likelihood of any misreading. (I have read many a sombre and critical account of poems that were intended ironically, even humorously.) The student will then avoid such statements as that made by the bishop who, after reading the first edition of Swift's *Gulliver's Travels*, pronounced it a little 'far-fetched' and for his part he 'did not believe a word of it'.

WRITTEN ANALYSIS: TWO SAMPLES

The following represents two pieces of actual poetry analysis. They are
not intended as 'model answers' to be directly copied. They are an attempt to pull together all the various aspects we have been examining
and to illustrate how they can be used in an integrated, structured,
'working' sample.

COMPOSED UPON WESTMINSTER BRIDGE

Earth has not anything to show more fair:
Dull would he be of soul who could pass by
A sight so touching in its majesty;
This City now doth, like a garment, wear
The beauty of the morning; silent, bare,   5
Ships, towers, domes, theatres, and temples lie
Open unto the fields, and to the sky;
All bright and glittering in the smokeless air.
Never did sun more beautifully steep
In his first splendour, valley, rock, or hill;   10
Ne'er saw I, never felt, a calm so deep!
The river glideth at his own sweet will:
Dear God! the very houses seem asleep;
And all that mighty heart is lying still.

William Wordsworth

In this poem, the poet is moved by the still, silent beauty of a city in
the early morning, before the bustle of its daily activity. Cities are usually seen as ugly, soulless places, yet here the poet celebrates a tranquil,
'majestic' beauty that is as compelling as the most beautiful 'natural'
landscape.

The poem is written in the form of a Petrarchan sonnet. The traditional octave/sestet division of this form allows the poet to describe the
view of the city in the octave, then shift the emphasis to compare this
beauty with that of Nature in the sestet. The tone of the poem suggests a
hushed, almost breathless admiration as the poet appears to have been
surprised by such a sudden vision of splendour. Occasionally the tone
becomes more emotional in its tribute to such beauty, as in lines 5–7.
This is aided by the rhythm of the poem, which alternates between emphasized, self-contained, one-line statements, such as:

Earth has not anything to show more fair:

or, even more pointedly, the final four lines of the poem, and a slight
quickening of pace through a series of 'run on' lines, such as lines 5–7, or

9–10. The prevailing atmosphere of calm, silent serenity also complements the effect.

The poem opens with an arresting, confident pronouncement in an 'end-stopped' line:

> Earth has not anything to show more fair:

The use of 'Earth' suggests the supreme quality of such beauty — a fact emphasized by the heavy rhythmic stress on 'Earth', 'anything' and 'fair' — by indicating the entire world. The other association of the word, that is, 'soil' and, by implication, Nature, prepares us for the later comparison with 'natural' beauty. Rhythmic devices are also interesting in the following two lines. By inverting normal word order, the word 'Dull' is particularly emphasized, while the enjambement effect of these lines helps to stress 'A sight so touching'. These lines are also linked by the rhyme, which produces a telling, compact effect. The repetition of the *s* sound helps convey the 'breathless' sense of admiration.

Line four introduces what the poet is describing and the 'City' is given added significance by the capital letter. The overall vision of beauty is seen in terms of a simile, a beauty that rests 'like a garment' over the entire city. 'Garment' suggests a comfortable, easy 'fit' — yet the word is more grand than say, 'clothing', and the beauty of the scene is enhanced by implications of resplendent finery. The details of the scene are presented in the form of a 'list' that gathers increasing momentum to convey the poet's sense of wonder. The description opens with two adjectives that describe the general scene, then a series of nouns that constitute its detail:

> silent, bare,
> Ships, towers, domes, theatres, and temples lie
> Open unto the fields, and to the sky.

The effect is further emphasized by the full, one-syllable rhyme of 'lie'/ 'sky'. Again it is the tone that conveys the feeling of admiration and beauty as 'towers, theatres' etc. do not normally strike us as 'poetically' beautiful, nor are they described in any detail. The octave closes with another pronounced, one-line statement:

> All bright and glittering in the smokeless air.

This has the effect of arresting the movement after the slight acceleration of the previous lines. Within the line, the rhythm accentuates 'bright', 'glittering' and 'smokeless', as much of the beauty of the scene is conveyed in terms of light. 'Smokeless' has a particularly still, pure, unpolluted quality and perhaps reminds us of how the scene will change once the day's 'smokey' industry begins. The rhyme that is rounded off here — 'bare/air' — also contributes a light, open feeling to the atmosphere.

The emphatic, decisive 'Never' effects the change in emphasis in the sestet. Now the poet compares the beauty before him to that of Nature.

Once more, normal word order is inverted and intensified to stress 'more beautifully'. The quality of the scene's beauty is again stressed in:

steep
In his first splendor, valley, rock, or hill;

'Steep' has a powerful, all-embracing quality. The enjambement here emphasizes 'In first splendour'. This may just mean no natural scene, in early morning sunlight, could appear more beautiful than the city does now. Yet by receiving such emphasis, there is perhaps a suggestion of hyperbole; that is, no scene, anywhere, since the first light of creation, could appear more beautiful. The listing of 'valley, rock, or hill' balances the details of the city in line six.

The use of emphatic negatives continues with the repetition of 'Ne'er' and 'never'. The rhythm of line eleven is particularly pointed and sharp:

Ne'er saw I, never felt, a calm so deep!

with each of the three phrases receiving telling emphasis, together with the exclamation mark. The tone becomes even more elevated through the use of four end-stopped lines that follow as separate, highlighted statements of wonder. The effect is further developed by the use of the rich, full quality of the rhyme — 'steep'/'deep'/'asleep'. 'Glideth' has a peaceful, fluid quality, a calmness aided by the river's moving at 'his own sweet will'. These subtle suggestions of personification (the sun is also seen as 'he' — i.e. 'his first splendor') suggest a gentle, living force beneath the entire scene. 'Dear God' suggests both intense exclamation and gratitude that such beauty exists. The hushed intensity of feeling continues with the 'very houses seem asleep', a feeling conveyed by the intensifier 'very' and the repetition of the *s* sound. It is the silent, still quality of the scene that is left as the final impression:

And all that mighty heart is lying still.

It is this unexpected silence and stillness that seems most to have surprised and touched the poet. This is, perhaps, natural as the city is normally associated with noise and crowds, a reminder of which lies in 'mighty heart'. It is on this note of contrast that the poem closes in a manner similar to that in which it opened — an emphatic, one-line pronouncement, delivered in a tone which now borders on incredulous wonder.

This poem seeks to convey the poet's feelings of wonder and admiration on being surprised by the tranquil beauty of the normally crowded, noisy city. Within the scope of the short sonnet form, the poem depends most on tone, rhythm and the interweaving, musical quality of its rhyme, rather than developed or elaborate use of imagery, to achieve this. The effective use of these devices enables us to share the poet's sense of wonder, even though we are not presented with any detailed illustrations of the scene itself.

RELIC

I found this jawbone at the sea's edge:
There, crabs, dogfish, broken by the breakers or tossed
To flap for half an hour and turn to a crust
Continue the beginning. The deeps are cold:
In that darkness camaraderie[1] does not hold: 5
Nothing touches but, clutching, devours. And the jaws,
Before they are satisfied or their stretched purpose
Slacken, go down jaws; go gnawn bare. Jaws
Eat and are finished and the jawbone comes to the beach:
This is the sea's achievement; with shells,   10
Vertebrae, claws, carapaces[2], skulls.
Time in the sea eats its tail, thrives, casts these
Indigestibles, the spars[3] of purposes
That failed far from the surface. None grow rich
In the sea. This curved jawbone did not laugh   15
But gripped, gripped and is now a cenotaph[4].

Ted Hughes

[1] comradeship
[2] shells of turtles, etc.
[3] ships' masts
[4] monument to the dead whose actual remains are elsewhere

In this poem, the poet observes the debris of remains of once living sea creatures that are found on any beach and is lead to contemplate the mysterious nature of life in the sea. The sea covers vast areas of the Earth's surface and was the original source of evolution for human life. By examining the quality of life beneath the oceans, the poet is able to suggest comparisons and implications that relate to human life.

The poem is written in free verse — although it has a certain regularity of line-length that is close to blank verse. It also makes occasional — and effective — use of rhyme. Free verse here allows the poet a freedom for subtle rhythmic variety. It also complements the poem's quietly contemplative, detached, 'flat', low-key, and occasionally harsh tone. The comparative regularity of lengthy lines produces an overall rhythm that is slow and steady, punctuated by pauses that suggest the gradual unfolding of the poet's thoughts, yet it is occasionally quickened for a particular effect.

The poem's opening line, a simple, complete, one-line statement, conveys the impression of the poet talking to us directly. The word 'edge' has a hard, precarious quality (which, say, 'shore' or 'beach' would not carry) that prepares us for the cold, harsh, mysterious atmosphere that dominates the poem. This dramatic opening focuses our attention on the skeletal remains and develops the idea of the poem's title — the implications of which will be exploited, ironically, later in the poem ('relic' being not just the physical remains, but more specifically the remains of a special, usually holy, person). The following lines:

> There, crabs, dogfish, broken by the breakers or tossed
> To flap for half an hour and turn to a crust
> Continue the beginning

are rich in subtle detail. The creatures, 'crabs' and 'dogfish', are particularly unglamorous, both in their names and as creatures. The sound of the breaking waves is echoed in the alliteration of 'broken by the breakers' and the repetition of the *s* sound. The rolling of the waves is suggested by the use of enjambement, particularly in the rhythm of 'or tossed/To flap for half an hour'. The repetition of the hard, dry *k* ('crabs', 'breakers', 'crust' etc.) and *t* sounds recalls the features of the bones that are washed up on the shore. For all the life these creatures once possessed, they can now do no more than 'flap' — a pointedly futile and insignificant movement, and that for a mere 'half an hour'. 'Continue the beginning' has a rich, perhaps sententious, ring to it and introduces the concept of eternal, circular continuity that will be developed later in the poem.

Following this, the short half line 'The deeps are cold' arrests the rhythm and is heavily emphasized. This creates an atmosphere of alienation and possibly menace; 'deeps' has a powerful, almost onomatopoeic, evocative quality here. This statement is developed in the following line and the two lines are effectively locked together by the unexpected, yet effective use of rhyme. As such, the lines form a couplet and the rhyme itself 'cold/hold' has a deep, echoing quality about it. The introduction of 'darkness' deepens the impressions of cold and mystery. The phrase 'camaraderie does not hold' not only suggests an absence of 'fellowship'; its associations relate specifically to warm and hearty comradeship — against which the life in the sea stands in chilling contrast.

'Nothing touches but, clutching, devours' is an effective example of how poetry can gain an effect of intensity through condensing grammar and word order. The rhythm here is broken and hurried to suggest the sudden struggle as one creature of the sea 'devours' another. There is an aural impression of the snapping of jaws in the syllable repetition of 'touches but clutching'. The total isolation of sea creatures is conveyed by the fact that nothing 'touches' — there are no gestures of warmth, affection or concern here. Nor do the creatures simply 'eat'; there is a brutal, voracious quality to the word 'devours'.

The rhythm preceding these lines (lines 4–6) is broken, disjointed. Yet as the idea develops and the predator of one fish quickly becomes the victim of another, the rhythm flows more freely to convey the speed with which all this takes place:

> And the jaws,
> Before they are satisfied or their stretched purpose
> Slacken, go down jaws.

Again there is an effective, onomatopoeic quality behind 'stretched' and 'slacken' and the quick movement of the run on line also links them as alliteration. Even before these creatures have been satisfied by their food they themselves become food for others as they 'go down jaws' — a phrase which admirably captures the simple, matter-of-fact tone of the poem's diction. This is emphasized by 'go gnawn bare', where the twisting combination of vowel sounds conveys the chewing movement of the jaws.

The use of blank, flat statement continues in:

> Jaws
> Eat and are finished and the jawbone comes to the beach.

The use of 'and' here suggests the simple, irrefutable inevitability of it all, almost with the tone of a child's recitation. The continued use of 'jaws' has by now developed to stress the impersonality of the life in the sea, where the creatures are not seen as creatures or given a name. 'This is the sea's achievement' is another resonant phrase that recalls 'Continue the beginning'. The use of 'achievement' appears, at first, ironic, even bitter, yet the idea is developed differently as the poem continues. The first section of the poem concludes with the dull, mundane listing of the sea's 'trophies', presented simply in their cold, biologically technical 'hardness':

> with shells,
> Vertebrae, claws, carapaces, skulls.

The break in the verse allows us to pause before the poet draws together the final observations on his theme. The first section of the poem outlines the characteristics of marine life. Now the poet considers the implications. This section opens with a striking image, that of the sea 'eating its tail'. This is perhaps the most powerful of the poem's constant images of 'eating' ('devour', 'gnawn', 'go down jaws' etc.). Specifically it is the concept of 'time' that is used to suggest the eternal, recurring continuity of life under the sea. The possibly negative, or futile aspect of the image of trying to eat one's tail is undercut by the next word 'thrives' — a word that not only suggests 'continues' but also 'flourishes successfully'. Perhaps it thrives because the natural laws are followed unquestioningly and the creatures do not struggle against the inevitable. The enjambement of 'casts these/Indigestibles' produces a rhythmic stress, a 'casting up' into focus, on 'Indigestibles'. The word itself has a hard quality to it, with its difficult, disjointed combination of syllables.

There is a subtle 'human' element within the poem, in the 'I' of the opening line and 'camaraderie', which is now brought more sharply into focus. The use of 'spars', the poles that form a ship's mast, by implication, brings mankind within the poem's scope, perhaps with the suggestion that, within the vast 'ocean' of time and eternity, all life comes to this same conclusion. There is something desolate and hopeless about the fact that such 'failures' occur 'far from the surface'.

The poet becomes more specific in relating life beneath the sea to human life on land when he states:

> None grow rich
> In the sea.

The enjambement particularly emphasizes the opening of the following line and in this way highlights the contrast even more. The poet could be suggesting here that, for all its seeming harshness, life in the sea is somehow more 'in tune' with the natural laws of the universe. Sea creatures are obsessed only with survival and not such 'trivial' things as the accumulation of wealth. As the poem has observed the circular continuity of existence in the sea, so it closes by taking us back to the actual jawbone — our original starting-point:

> This curved jawbone did not laugh
> But gripped, gripped and is now a cenotaph.

The rhyme here is effective with its satisfying 'finality'. Again, 'laughter' invites the comparison with human existence. The poet's attitude to this comparison now appears ambiguous. Yet perhaps he is stating that if life in the sea avoids the trivial and negative aspects of human life, it also lacks its 'camaraderie', its 'touching' and its 'laughter'. The repetition of 'gripped', with its 'aural' impact and associations of relentless ferocity, recall the conditions of sea existence outlined earlier. 'Cenotaph' becomes a metaphor that is again associated with death. Although a cenotaph is to commemorate those whose remains are lost — a particularly tragic fate — it is not used here in an emotional or sad way. It stands as a fitting end to the poem's bleak and sombre tone and atmosphere.

This poem succeeds in conveying the poet's thoughts about the nature of existence beneath the sea. The use of powerful, predominantly tactile images vividly conveys the poet's impressions of that existence. Subtle effects of rhythm and use of aural devices complement the descriptions. The entire poem is locked in a cold and heavy tone and atmosphere. The difficulties in the poem lie in trying to assess what the poet feels towards his subject, especially when he relates this existence to that of mankind. We have already noticed a certain ambiguity in the contrasts. At times the poet seems to be relating the two forms of life together — with the implication that all life comes to such a fate. Or perhaps he is merely concerned with pointing out two different forms of existence. The nature of existence in the sea is not 'condemned', in spite of its harsh brutality at times. The detached manner of the poet's presentation prevents the treatment from becoming sad or gloomy. In fact the poet pays tribute to the 'continuity' and implied 'harmony' of this existence. This may be the key to the comparison with human life, which struggles after illusions of progress and change and therefore loses the harmonious 'continuity' of the natural, rather than man-made, laws.

Here, then, are two examples of poetry appreciation 'in action'. The above analyses do not say all that may be observed in the two poems, but they do illustrate the sort of depth and amount of detail that can be dealt with in the course of a timed analysis.

CHAPTER 12

POEMS FOR ANALYSIS

The following poems constitute a wide variety of poetry, selected from different periods of English poetry, both in terms of form and theme. The poems may be used for either discussion or written analysis. Poems 1–20 may be looked at individually, while exercises 21–24 offer practice in comparing poems. Exercises 24–30 are taken from previous Advanced Level English examination papers, selected from the Cambridge Overseas papers.

1.   WHEN YOU ARE OLD

When you are old and gray and full of sleep,
And nodding by the fire, take down this book,
And slowly read, and dream of the soft look
Your eyes had once, and of their shadows deep;

How many loved your moments of glad grace,   5
And loved your beauty with love false or true,
But one man loved the pilgrim soul in you,
And loved the sorrows of your changing face;

And bending down beside the glowing bars,
Murmur, a little sadly, how love fled   10
And paced upon the mountains overhead
And hid his face amid a crowd of stars.

2.   A NEGRO WOMAN

carrying a bunch of marigolds
     wrapped
          in an old newspaper:
She carries them upright,
     bareheaded,   5
          the bulk
of her thighs
     causing her to waddle
          as she walks
looking into   10
     the store window which she passes
          on her way.
What is she
     but an ambassador
          from another world   15
a world of pretty marigolds
     of two shades
          which she announces
not knowing what she does
     other   20
          than walk the streets
holding the flowers upright
     as a torch
          so early in the morning.

3.   SEA MEMORY

Deep in the hills, in the tree country,
I have brought memories of the sea country.

To my mountain door
Comes the surf's deep-muted roar.
Here is a feather   5
Blown by monsoonal weather
From a reef-bird's breast
That came to rest
On the storm-swept beach.
As songs from ships and sailors' graves   10
The tranquil speech
Of wind and waves
Invades my hills.
A pink-flushed fluted shell
Would passionately tell   15
Of coral pools and tides,
A far ship's bell,
And hopes the sea alone fulfils.

Here with the birds and Morning Star
My constant calendar,   20
The pea-field's bloom, pear-tree's awakening,
The season's change
From lambing-time to marketing —
The whole year's range —
I still have memories of tropic seas.   25
Tall trunks of carabeen,
The harbour-maze of forest trees,
For me can only mean
The stately masts of Timor sloops;
Each couple-contoured cloud recalls   30
Loose upper-canvas snared in ropes
Or straining to the sudden squalls.
And as the rain my mountain lashes
These memories stab like lighthouse flashes.

Time keeps for me few souvenirs   35
More pungent than those sea-lived years.

4.   PIANO

Softly, in the dusk, a woman is singing to me;
Taking me back down the vista of years, till I see
A child sitting under the piano, in the boom of the tingling
    strings
And pressing the small, poised feet of a mother who smiles as   5
    she sings.

In spite of myself, the insidious mastery of song
Betrays me back, till the heart of me weeps to belong
To the old Sunday evenings at home, with winter outside
And hymns in the cozy parlour, the tinkling piano our guide.   10

So now it is vain for the singer to burst into clamour
With the great black piano appassionato[1]. The glamour
Of childish days is upon me, my manhood is cast
Down in the flood of remembrance, and I weep like a child for
    the past.   15

[1] musical term meaning 'with feeling'

5.   JOURNEY OF THE MAGI[1]

"A cold coming we had of it,
Just the worst time of year
For a journey, and such a long journey:

The ways deep and the weather sharp,
The very dead of winter."   5
And the camels galled, sore-footed, refractory[2],
Lying down in the melted snow.
There were times we regretted
The summer palaces on slopes, the terraces,
And the silken girls bringing sherbet.[3].   10
Then the camel men cursing and grumbling
And running away, and wanting their liquor and women,
And the night-fires going out, and the lack of shelters,
And the cities hostile and the towns unfriendly
And the villages dirty and charging high prices: 15
A hard time we had of it.
At the end we preferred to travel all night,
Sleeping in snatches,
With the voices singing in our ears, saying
That this was all folly.   20
Then at dawn we came down to a temperate valley,
Wet, below the snow line, smelling of vegetation;
With a running stream and a water mill beating the darkness,
And three trees on the low sky,
And an old white horse galloped away in the meadow.   25
Then we came to a tavern with vine-leaves over the lintel,
Six hands at an open door dicing for pieces of silver,
And feet kicking the empty wineskins.
But there was no information, and so we continued
And arrived at evening, not a moment too soon   30
Finding the place; it was (you may say) satisfactory."
All this was a long time ago, I remember,
And I would do it again, but set down
This set down
This: were we led all that way for   35
Birth or Death? There was a Birth, certainly,
We had evidence and no doubt. I had seen birth and death,
But had thought they were different; this Birth was
Hard and bitter agony for us, like Death, our death.
We returned to our places, these Kingdoms,   40
But no longer at ease here, in the old dispensation[4],
With an alien people clutching their gods.
I should be glad of another death.

---

[1] the three wise men who journeyed to do homage to the birth of Christ
   One of them is recalling the experience in this poem.
[2] stubborn, unmanageable
[3] sweet flavoured drink
[4] manner, order

6.   THE LATEST DECALOGUE[1]

Thou shalt have one God only; who
Would be at the expense of two?
No graven images may be
Worshiped, except the currency.
Swear not at all; for, for thy curse   5
Thine enemy is none the worse.
At church on Sunday to attend
Will serve to keep the world thy friend.
Honour thy parents; that is, all
From whom advancement may befall.   10
Thou shalt not kill; but need'st not strive
Officiously to keep alive.
Do not adultery commit;
Advantage rarely comes of it.
Thou shalt not steal; an empty feat,   15
When it's so lucrative to cheat.
Bear not false witness; let the lie
Have time on its own wings to fly.
Thou shalt not covet, but tradition
Approves all form of competition.   20
The sum of all is, thou shalt love,
If anybody, God above:
At any rate shall never labour
More than thyself to love thy neighbour.

[1] the Ten Commandments

7.   AN IRISH AIRMAN FORESEES HIS DEATH

I know that I shall meet my fate
Somewhere among the clouds above;
Those that I fight I do not hate,
Those that I guard I do not love;
My country is Kiltartan Cross[1],   5
My countrymen Kiltartan's poor,
No likely end could bring them loss
Or leave them happier than before.
Nor law, nor duty bade me fight,
Nor public men, nor cheering crowds,   10
A lonely impulse of delight
Drove to this tumult in the clouds;
I balanced all, brought all to mind,
The years to come seemed waste of breath,
A waste of breath the years behind   15
In balance with this life, his death.

[1] district in Ireland

8.   All the world's a stage,
And all the men and women merely players:
They have their exits and their entrances;
And one man in his time plays many parts,
His acts being seven ages. At first the infant,   5
Mewling and puking in the nurse's arms.
Then the whining school-boy, with his satchel
And shining morning face, creeping like snail
Unwillingly to school. And then the lover,
Sighing like furnace, with a woeful ballad   10
Made to his mistress' eyebrow. Then a soldier,
Full of strange oaths, and bearded like the bard,
Jealous in honour, sudden and quick in quarrel,
Seeking the bubble reputation
Even in the cannon's mouth. And then the justice,   15
In fair round belly with good capon lined,
With eyes severe and beard of formal cut,
Full of wise saws and modern instances;
And so he plays his part. The sixth age shifts
Into the lean and slipper'd pantaloon,   20
With spectacles on nose and pouch on side,
His youthful hose, well saved, a world too wide
For his shrunk shank; and his big manly voice,
Turning again toward childish treble, pipes
And whistles in his sound. Last scene of all,   25
That ends this strange eventful history,
Is second childishness and mere oblivion,
Sans[1] teeth, sans eyes, sans taste, sans everything.

(Speech by Jaques in Shakespeare's *As You Like It*)

[1] without

9.   DEATH THE LEVELLER

The glories of our blood and state
    Are shadows, not substantial things;
There is no armour against Fate;
    Death lays his icy hand on kings:
      Sceptre and Crown   5
      Must tumble down,
    And in the dust be equal made
With the poor crooked scythe and spade.

Some men with swords may reap the field,
    And plant fresh laurels where they kill: 10
But their strong nerves at last must yield;
    They tame but one another still:

Early or late
They stoop to fate,
And must give up their murmuring breath   15
When they, pale captives, creep to death.

The garlands wither on your brow;
   Then boast no more your mighty deeds!
Upon Death's purple altar now
   See where the victor-victim bleeds.   20
      Your heads must come
      To the cold tomb:
Only the actions of the just
Smell sweet and blossom in their dust.

10.   DO NOT GO GENTLE INTO THAT GOOD NIGHT

Do not go gentle into that good night,
Old age should burn and rave at close of day;
Rage, rage against the dying of the light.

Though wise men at their end know dark is right,
Because their words had forked no lightening they   5
Do not go gentle into that good night.

Good men, the last wave by, crying how bright
Their frail deeds might have danced in a green bay,
Rage, rage against the dying of the light.

Wild men who caught and sang the sun in flight,   10
And learn, too late, they grieved it on its way,
Do not go gentle into that good night.

Grave men, near death, who see with blinding sight
Blind eyes could blaze like meteors and be gay,
Rage, rage against the dying of the light.   15

And you, my father, there on the sad height,
Curse, bless, me now with your fierce tears, I pray.
Do not go gentle into that good night.
Rage, rage against the dying of the light.

11.   LOVE'S COMING

Quietly as rosebuds
   Talk to thin air
Love came so lightly
   I knew not he was there.

Quietly as lovers   5

Creep at the middle noon,
   Softly as players tremble
     In the tears of a tune;

Quietly as lilies
     Their faint vows declare,   10
Came the shy pilgrim:
     I knew not he was there.

Quietly as tears fall
     On a warm sin,
Softly as griefs call   15
     In a violin;

Without hail or tempest,
     Blue sword or flame,
Love came so lightly
     I knew not that he came.   20

12.   A GENTLEMAN

"He has robbed two clubs. The judge at Salisbury
Can't give him more than he undoubtedly
Deserves. The scoundrel! Look at his photograph!
A lady-killer! Hanging's too good by half
For such as he." So said the stranger, one   5
With crimes yet undiscovered or undone.
But at the inn the Gypsy dame began:
"Now he was what I call a gentleman.
He went along with Carric, and when she
Had a baby he paid up so readily   10
His half a crown. Just like him. A crown'd have been
More like him. For I never knew him mean.
Oh! but he was such a nice gentleman. Oh!
Last time we met he said if me and Joe
Was anywhere near we must be sure and call.   15
He put his arms around our Amos all
As if he were his own son. I pray God
Save him from justice! Nicer man never trod[1]".

[1] i.e. on earth

13.   THE SHADOW ON THE STONE

     I went by the Druid stone
     That broods in the garden white and lone,
And I stopped and looked at the shifting shadows

That at some moments fall thereon
From the tree hard by with a rhythmic swing,   5
And they shaped in my imagining
To the shade that a well-known head and shoulders
Threw there when she was gardening.

    I thought her behind my back,
    Yea, her I long had learned to lack,   10
And I said: "I am sure you are standing behind me,
    Though how do you get into this old track?"
    And there was no sound but the fall of a leaf
    As a sad response; and to keep down grief
I would not turn my head to discover   15
    That there was nothing in my belief.

    Yet I wanted to look and see
    That nobody stood at the back of me;
But I thought once more: "Nay, I'll not unvision
    A shape which, somehow, there may be".   20
    So I went on softly from the glade,
    And left her behind me throwing her shade,
As she were indeed an apparition —
    My head unturned lest my dream should fade.

14.   LIGHTS OUT

I have come to the borders of sleep,
The unfathomable deep
Forest where all must lose
Their way, however straight,
Or winding, soon or late;   5
They cannot choose.

Many a road and track
That, since the dawn's first crack,
Up to the forest brink,
Deceived the travellers,   10
Suddenly now blurs,
And in they sink.

Here love ends —
Despair, ambition ends:
All pleasure and all trouble,   15
Although most sweet or bitter,
Here ends in sleep that is sweeter
Than tasks most noble.

There is not any book
Or face of dearest look   20

That I would not turn from now
To go into the unknown
I must enter, and leave, alone,
I know not how.

The tall forest towers;   25
Its cloudy foliage lowers
Ahead, shelf above shelf;
Its silence I hear and obey
That I may lose my way
And myself.   30

15.   THE SOLITARY REAPER

Behold her, single in the field,
Yon solitary Highland Lass!
Reaping and singing by herself;
Stop here, or gently pass!
Alone she cuts and binds the grain,   5
And sings a melancholy strain;
O listen! for the Vale profound
Is overflowing with the sound.

No Nightingale did ever chaunt
More welcome notes to weary bands   10
Of travellers in some shady haunt,
Among Arabian sands:
A voice so thrilling ne'er was heard
In Spring-time from the Cuckoo-bird,
Breaking the silence of the seas   15
Among the farthest Hebrides[1].

Will no one tell me what she sings? —
Perhaps the plaintive numbers flow
For old, unhappy, far-off things,
And battles long ago: 20
Or is it some more humble lay,
Familiar matter of today?
Some natural sorrow, loss, or pain,
That has been and may be again!

Whate'er the theme, the Maiden sang   25
As if her song could have no ending;
I saw her singing at her work,
And o'er the sickle bending; —
I listened till I had my fill;
And, as I mounted up the hill,   30
The music in my heart I bore,

Long after it was heard no more.

¹ remote islands off Scottish coast

16.   A BLIND CHILD

Her baby brother laughed last night,
    The blind child asked her mother why;
    It was the light that caught his eye.
Would she might laugh to see that light!

The presence of a stiffened corpse   5
    Is sad enough; but, to my mind,
    The presence of a child that's blind,
In a green garden, is far worse.

She felt my cloth — for worldly place;
    She felt my face — if I was good;   10
    My face lost more than half its blood,
For fear her hand would wrongly trace.

We're in the garden, where are bees
    And flowers, and birds, and butterflies;
    One greedy fledgling runs and cries   15
For all the food his parent sees!

I see them all: flowers of all kind,
    The sheep and cattle on the leas;
    The houses up the hills, the trees —
But I am dumb, for she is blind.   20

17.   No matter where; of comfort no man speak:
        Let's talk of graves, of worms, and epitaphs,
        Make dust our paper, and with rainy eyes
        Write sorrow on the bosom of the earth.
        Let's choose executors, and talk of wills: 5
        And yet not so; for what can we bequeathe,
        Save our deposed bodies to the ground? ....
        .... For God's sake let us sit upon the ground,
        And tell sad stories of the death of Kings:
        How some have been depos'd, some slain in war,
        Some haunted by the ghosts they have depos'd,
        Some poison'd by their wives, some sleeping kill'd,
        All murther'd. For within the hollow Crown
        That rounds the mortal temples of a King,
        Keeps Death his Court, and there the Antic sits   15
        Scoffing his state, and grinning at his pomp,

Allowing him a breath, a little scene,
To monarchise, be fear'd, and kill with looks,
Infusing him with self and vain conceit,
As if this flesh, which walls about our life,   20
Were brass impregnable: and humour'd thus,
Comes at the last, and with a little pin
Bores through his castle wall, and farewell King.

(Speech of the deposed king in Shakespeare's *Richard II*.)

18.   BEACH BURIAL

Softly and humbly to the Gulf of Arabs
The convoys of dead sailors come;
At night they sway and wander in the waters far under,
But morning rolls them in the foam.

Between the sob and clubbing of the gunfire   5
Someone, it seems, has time for this,
To pluck them from the shallows and bury them in burrows
And tread the sand upon their nakedness;

And each cross, the driven stake of tidewood,
Bears the last signature of men,   10
Written with such perplexity, with such bewildered pity,
The words choke as they begin —

'Unknown seaman' — the ghostly pencil
Wavers and fades, the purple drips,
The breath of the wet season has washed their inscriptions 15
As blue as drowned men's lips,

Dead seamen, gone in search of the same landfall,
Whether as enemies they fought,
Or fought with us, or neither; the sand joins them together,
Enlisted on the other front.   20

19.   FOLLOWER

My father worked with a horse-plough,
His shoulders globed like a full sail strung
Between the shafts and the furrow.
The horses strained at his clicking tongue.

An expert. He would set the wing   5
And fit the bright steel-pointed sock.
The sod rolled over without breaking.

At the headrig, with a single pluck

Of reins, the sweating team turned round
And back into the land. His eye   10
Narrowed and angled at the ground,
Mapping the furrow exactly.

I stumbled in his hob-nailed[1] wake,
Fell sometimes on the polished sod;
Sometimes he rode me on his back   15
Dipping and rising to his plod.

I wanted to grow up and plough,
To close one eye, stiffen my arm.
All I ever did was follow
In his broad shadow round the farm.   20

I was a nuisance, tripping, falling,
Yapping always. But today
It is my father who keeps stumbling
Behind me, and will not go away.

[1] heavy boot

20.   Somewhere I have never travelled, gladly beyond
       any experience, your eyes have their silence:
       in your most frail gesture are things which enclose me,
       or which I cannot touch because they are too near.

       Your slightest look easily will unclose me   5
       though I have closed myself as fingers,
       you open always petal by petal myself as Spring opens
       (touching skilfully, mysteriously) her first rose

       or if your wish be to close me, I and
       my life will shut very beautifully, suddenly,   10
       as when the heart of this flower imagines
       the snow carefully everywhere descending;

       nothing which we are to perceive in this world equals
       the power of your intense fragility: whose texture
       compels me with the colour of its countries,   15
       rendering death and forever with each breathing.

       (I do not know what it is about you that closes
       and opens; only something in me understands
       the voice of your eyes is deeper than all roses)
       nobody, not even the rain, has such small hands.   20

21. Compare and contrast the use the following two poems make of the lyric form.

A   TO ———

    Music, when soft voices die,
    Vibrates in the memory —
    Odors, when sweet violets sicken,
    Live within the sense they quicken.
    Rose leaves, when the rose is dead,   5
    Are heaped for the beloved's bed;
    And so thy thoughts[1], when thou art gone,
    Love itself shall slumber on.

   [1] i.e. my thoughts of thee

B   MAD SONG

    The wild winds weep,
        And the night is a-cold;
    Come hither, Sleep,
        And my griefs infold:
    But lo! the morning peeps   5
        Over the eastern steeps,
    And the rustling birds of dawn
    The earth do scorn.

    Lo! to the vault
        Of paved heaven,   10
    With sorrow fraught
        My notes are driven:
    They strike the ear of night,
        Make weep the eyes of day;
    They make mad the roaring winds,   15
        And the tempest play.

    Like a fiend in a cloud
        With howling woe,
    After night I do croud[1],
        And with night will go;   20
    I turn my back to the east,
    From whence comforts have increas'd;
    For light doth seize my brain
    With frantic pain.

   [1] call

22. Compare and contrast the way the following poems treat the theme of death.

A   FUNERAL BLUES

    Stop all the clocks, cut off the telephone;
    Prevent the dog from barking with a juicy bone;
    Silence the pianos, and with muffled drum
    Bring out the coffin, let the mourners come.

    Let aeroplanes circle a moaning overhead,   5
    Scribbling on the sky the message: "He is dead".
    Put crepe bows round the white necks of public doves;
    Let the traffic policemen wear black cotton gloves.

    He was my North, my South, and East, and West,
    My working week, and my Sunday rest;   10
    My noon, my midnight, my talk, my song;
    I thought that love could last forever: I was wrong.

    The stars are not wanted now, put out every one;
    Pack up the moon and dismantle the sun
    Pour away the ocean, and sweep up the wood: 15
    For nothing now can come to any good.

B   THERE'S BEEN A DEATH

    There's been a Death, in the Opposite House,
    As lately as Today —
    I know it, by the numb look
    Such Houses have — alway —

    The neighbours rustle in and out —   5
    The Doctor — drives away —
    A window opens like a Pod —
    Abrupt — mechanically —

    Somebody flings a Mattress out —
    The Children hurry by —   10
    They wonder if it died — on that —
    I used to — when a Boy —

    The Minister — goes stiffly in —
    As if the House were His —
    And he owned all the Mourners — now —   15
    And little Boys — besides —

    And then the Milliner[1]— and the Man
    Of the Appalling Trade —
    To take the measure of the House —
    There'll be that Dark Parade —   20

Of Tassles — and of Coaches — soon —
It's easy as a Sign —
The Intuition of the News —
In just a Country Town.

¹ hat-maker

23. Compare and contrast the following poets' recollections of people they once knew.

A   HE   WAS

    a brown old man with a green thumb:
    I can remember the screak on stones of his hoe,
    The chug, choke, and high madrigal wheeze
    Of the spray-cart bumping below
    The sputtery leaves of the apple trees,   5
    But he was all but dumb

    Who filled some quarter of the day with sound
    All of my childhood long. For all I heard
    Of all his labours, I can now recall
    Never a single word   10
    Until he went in the dead of fall
    To the drowsy underground,

    Having planted a young orchard with so great care
    In that last year that none was lost, and May
    Aroused them all, the leaves saying the land's   15
    Praise for the livening clay,
    And the found voice of his buried hands
    Rose in the sparrowy air.

B   THE LAST MYSTERY

    He knew that coastline — no man better —
    Knew all its rocks and currents, like the veins
    And knuckles on the brown back of his hand;
    The leap-frog rollers and tall tons that batter
    Boat-rib and man-rib into grains   5
    Of indistinguishable sand:
    He had known them all since he could stand.

    A shanty¹ was his earliest lullaby,
    The beach his back-yard, flotsam all his toys.
    He was admitted to the mystery   10
    Of tides; the wind's writing on the sky;
    Could out-sail, out-dive, out-swim boys
    Older by half; was known to save
    Many from the sabre-toothed, man-eating wave.

Knowing so well the temper of that coast,   15
And all subaqueous[2] hazards of the sea,
What voice, thought, impulse lugged him from his ale
(When every flag was fighting with a mast
And waves kicked bollards off the quay),
To match his Lilliputian[3] sail   20
Against the wrestling muscles of the gale?

Only the lemming[4] knows: his friends knew only
Boat-rib and man-rib littered the long shore
Many tides after. I declare he fell
Like a pearl-dazzled diver through the sea   25
To that last mystery on its floor;
Whose is the heart-beat under the swell,
The hand that turns the whirlpool and the shell?

[1] sea song
[2] underwater
[3] Lilliput was the land of the very small in Swift's *Gulliver's Travels*
[4] small arctic rodents that are reputed to rush each year headlong into the
sea and drown

24. Compare and contrast the attitudes expressed in the following two
    poems towards the city. You should consider the imagery of the city,
    and what purpose it serves.

A   Dark house, by which once more I stand
         Here in the long unlovely street,
         Doors, where my heart was used to beat
     So quickly,waiting for a hand,

     A hand that can be clasp'd no more —   5
         Behold me, for I cannot sleep,
         And like a guilty thing I creep
     At earliest morning to the door.

     He is not here; but far away
         The noise of life begins again,   10
         And ghastly thro' the drizzling rain
     On the bald street breaks the blank day.

B   Side by side through the streets at midnight,
     Roaming together,
     Through the tumultuous night of London,
     In the miraculous April weather.

     Roaming together under the gaslight,   5
     Day's work over,

How the Spring calls to us, here in the city
Calls to the heart from the heart of a lover!

Cool the wind blows, fresh in our faces,
Cleansing, entrancing,   10
After the heat and the fumes and the footlights,
Where you dance and I watch your dancing.

Good it is to be here together,
Good to be roaming,
Even in London, even at midnight,   15
Lover-like in a lover's gloaming.

You the dancer and I the dreamer,
Children together,
Wandering lost in the night of London,
In the miraculous April weather.   20

(Cambridge, 1973)

25.
A   THE VOICE

Woman much missed, how you call to me, call to me,
Saying that now you are not as you were
When you had changed from the one who was all to me,
But as at first, when our day was fair.

Can it be you that I hear? Let me view you, then,   5
Standing as when I drew near to the town
Where you would wait for me: yes, as I knew you then,
Even to the original air-blue gown!

Or is it only the breeze, in its listlessness
Travelling across the wet mead to me here,   10
You being ever dissolved to existlessness,
Heard no more again far or near?

    Thus I faltering forward,
    Leaves around me falling,
Wind oozing thin through the thorn from norward,   15
    And the woman calling.

B   LISTENING

I listen to the stillness of you,
    My dear, among it all;
I feel your silence touch my words as I talk
    And hold them in thrall.

My words fly off a forge   5
    The length of a spark;

I see the silence easily sip them
   Up in the dark.

The lark sings loud and glad.
   Yet I am not loth   10
That silence should take the song and the bird
   And lose them both.

A train goes roaring south,
   The steam-flag flowing;
I see the stealthy shadow of silence   15
   Alongside going.

And off the forge of the world
   Whirling in the draught of life
Go myriad sparks of people, filling
   The night with strife.   20

Yet they never change the darkness
   Nor blench it with noise;
Alone on the perfect silence
   The stars are buoys.

(i) Compare the relationship between the speaker and the woman addressed in each of these poems.

(ii) By what means, and with what success, does each poem convey a sense of this relationship? You should comment especially on the tone of voice, turn of phrase, imagery and rhythm, including the movement of each poem as a whole.

(Cambridge, 1974)

26.

A   THE WILD SWANS AT COOLE

The trees are in their autumn beauty,
The woodland paths are dry,
Under the October twilight the water
Mirrors a still sky;
Upon the brimming water among the stones   5
Are nine-and-fifty swans.

The nineteenth autumn has come upon me
Since first I made my count;
I saw, before I had well finished,
All suddenly mount   10
And scatter wheeling in great broken rings
Upon their clamorous wings.

I have looked upon those brilliant creatures,
And now my heart is sore.

All's changed since I, hearing at twilight,   15
The first time on this shore,
The bell-beat of their wings above my head,
Trod with a lighter tread.

Unwearied still, lover by lover,
They paddle in the cold   20
Companionable streams or climb the air;
Their hearts have not grown old;
Passion or conquest, wander where they will,
Attend upon them still.

But now they drift on the still water,   25
Mysterious, beautiful;
Among what rushes will they build,
By what lake's edge or pool
Delight men's eyes when I awake some day
To find they have flown away.   30

HAWK ROOSTING

I sit in the top of the wood, my eyes closed.
Inaction, no falsifying dream
Between my hooked head and hooked feet:
Or in sleep rehearse perfect kills and eat.

The convenience of the high trees!   5
The air's buoyancy and the sun's ray
Are of advantage to me;
And the earth's face upward for my inspection.

My feet are locked upon the rough bark.
It took the whole of Creation   10
To produce my foot, my each feather;
Now I hold Creation in my foot

Or fly up, and revolve it all slowly —
I kill where I please because it is all mine.
There is no sophistry in my body: 15
My manners are tearing off heads —

The allotment of death.
For the one path of my flight is direct
Through the bones of the living.
No arguments assert my right: 20

The sun is behind me.
Nothing has changed since I began.
My eye has permitted no change.
I am going to keep things like this.

(i) Compare the attitudes to the natural world expressed in each poem.
(ii) How successfully does the language of each poem convey its meaning?

(Cambridge, 1975)

27.

A   THE SCHOOL BOY

I love to rise in a summer morn
When the birds sing on every tree;
The distant huntsman winds his horn,
And the sky-lark sings with me.
O! what sweet company.   5

But to go to school in a summer morn,
O! it drives all joy away;
Under a cruel eye outworn
The little ones spend the day
In sighing and dismay.   10

Ah! then at times I drooping sit,
And spend many an anxious hour,
Nor in my book can I take delight,
Nor sit in learning's bower,
Worn thro' with the dreary shower.   15

How can the bird that is born for joy
Sit in a cage and sing?
How can a child when fears annoy
But droop his tender wing
And forget his youthful spring?   20

O! father and mother, if buds are nip'd
And blossoms blown away,
And if the tender plants are strip'd
Of their joy in the springing day,
By sorrow and care's dismay,   25

How shall the summer arise in joy,
Or the summer fruits appear?
Or how shall we gather what griefs destroy,
Or bless the mellowing year
When the blasts of winter appear?   30

B   A YOUNG GIRL

I search in vain your childlike face to see
The thoughts that hide behind the words you say;
I hear them singing, but close-shut from me
Dream the enchanted woods through which they stray.
Cheek, lip, and brow — I glance from each to each,   5

And watch that light-winged Mercury, your hand;
And sometimes when brief silence falls on speech
I seem your hidden self to understand.

Mine a dark fate. Behind his iron bars
The captive broods, with ear and heart a-strain   10
For jangle of key, for glimpse of moon or stars,
Grey shaft of daylight, sighing of the rain.
Life built these walls. Past all my dull surmise
Must burn the inward innocence of your eyes.

(i) Compare the attitudes towards childhood expressed in each poem.
(ii) How successfully does each poem convey its meaning? You should pay
special attention to rhythm, phrasing and tone of voice, commenting
on the movement of each poem as a whole.

(Cambridge, 1976).

28. Write a critical essay comparing the following two poems. In your
answer you should pay attention to the language of the poems, especially rhythm and phrasing.

A   STILL-LIFE

Through the open French window the warm sun
lights up the polished breakfast-table, laid
round a bowl of crimson roses, for one —
a service of Worcester porcelain, arrayed
near it a melon, peaches, figs, small hot   5
rolls in a napkin, fairy rack of toast,
butter in ice, high silver coffee pot,
and, heaped on a salver, the morning's post.

She comes over the lawn, the young heiress,
from her early walk in her garden-wood   10
feeling that life's a table set to bless
her delicate desires with all that's good,

that even the unopened future lies
like a love-letter, full of sweet surprise.

B   THE AGED LOVER DISCOURSES IN THE FLAT STYLE

There are, perhaps, whom passion gives a grace,
Who fuse and part as dancers on the stage,
But that is not for me, not at my age,
Not with bony shoulders and fat face.
Yet in my clumsiness I found a place   5
And use for passion: with it I ignore

My gaucheries and yours, and feel no more
The awkwardness of the absurd embrace.

It is a pact men make, and seal in flesh,
To be so busy with their own desires   10
Their loves may be as busy with their own,
And not in union. Though the two enmesh
Like gears in motion, each with each conspires
To be at once together and alone.

(Cambridge, 1978).

29. Write a critical comparison of the following two poems. You should
    pay special attention to the rhythm and movement of each poem as a
    whole.

A   OLD COUNTRYSIDE

Beyond the hour we counted rain that fell
On the slant shutter, all has come to proof.
The summer thunder, like a wooden bell,
Rang in the storm above the mansard roof,

And mirrors cast the cloudy day along   5
The attic floor; wind made the cupboards creak.
You braced against the wall to make it strong,
A shell against your cheek.

Long since, we pulled brown oak-leaves to the ground
In a winter of dry trees; we heard the cock   10
Shout its unplaceable cry, the axe's sound
Delay a moment after the axe's stroke.

Far back, we saw, in the stillest of the year,
The scrawled vine shudder, and the rose-branch show
Red to the thorns, and, sharp as sight can bear,   15
The thin hound's body arched against the snow.

B   THE MEDIUM

My answer would have to be music
which is always undeniable, since in my
silence, which you question, is only a landscape

of water, old trees and a few irresolute
birds. The weather is also inconstant.   5
Sometimes the light is golden, the leaves unseasonable.

And sometimes the ice is red, and the moon
hangs over it, peeled, like a chinese fruit.
I am sorry not to be more articulate.

When I try, the words turn ugly as rats and   10
disorder everything, I cannot be quiet,
I want so much to be quiet and loving

If only you wanted that. My sharpest thoughts
wait like assassins always in the dry wheat. They
chat and grin. Perhaps you should talk to them?

(Cambridge, 1979).

30. Write a critical comparison of the following two poems. You should
    pay close attention to the rhythm and movement of each poem as a
    whole, showing how the theme of the city is presented in each poem.

A   LONDON

I wander thro' each charter'd street,
Near where the charter'd Thames does flow,
And mark in every face I meet
Marks of weakness, marks of woe.

In every cry of every Man,   5
In every Infant's cry of fear,
In every voice, in every ban,
The mind-forg'd manacles I hear.

How the Chimney-sweeper's cry
Every black'ning Church appalls;
And the hapless Soldier's sigh   10
Runs in blood down Palace walls.

But most thro' midnight streets I hear
How the youthful Harlot's curse
Blasts the new born Infant's tear,   15
And blights with plagues the Marriage hearse.

B   WAITING

Within unfriendly walls
    We starve — or starve by stealth.
Oxen fatten in their stalls;
    You guard the harrier's health:
They never can be criminals,   5
    And can't compete for wealth.
        From the mansion and the palace
            Is there any help or hail
        For the tenants of the alleys,
            Of the workhouse and the jail?   10

Though land awaits our toil,

> And earth half-empty rolls,
> Cumberers of English soil,
>   We cringe for orts[1] and doles —
> Prosperity's accustomed foil, 15
>   Millions of useless souls.
>   In the gutters and the ditches
>   Human vermin festering lurk —
>   We, the rust upon your riches;
>   We, the flaw in all your work. 20

> Come down from where you sit;
>   We look to you for aid.
> Take us from the miry pit,
>   And lead us undismayed:
> Say, "Even you, outcast, unfit, 25
>   Forward with sword and spade!"
>   And myriads of us idle
>   Would thank you through our tears,
>   Though you drove us with a bridle,
>   And a whip about our ears! 30

> From cloudy cape to cape
>   The teeming waters seethe;
> Golden grain and purple grape
>   The regions overwreathe.
> Will no one help us to escape? 35
>   We scarce have room to breathe.
>   You might try to understand us:
>   We are waiting night and day
>   For a captain to command us,
>   And the word we must obey. 40

(Cambridge, 1980)

[1] left-overs

CHAPTER 13

GLOSSARY

Alliteration	The repetition of the same consonant sound, especially at the beginning of words
Allusion	Reference to a person, place, or event with which the reader is assumed to be familiar
Ambiguity	This signifies more than one meaning or interpretation is possible
Ambivalence	This signifies more than one possible attitude is being displayed by the poet towards his theme.
Apostrophe	Direct address to a person, or place, or an abstract idea (i.e. 'Duty', 'Love') personified
Archaic	Language that is no longer in use in the sense in which it is presented
Assonance	Repetition of similar vowel sounds
Atmosphere	The mood prevailing in the poem
Bathos	Anti-climax — whether deliberate, or unintentional
Cacophony	Use of harsh, or unpleasant sounds
Cliché	A once powerful or effective phrase (or image) that has become tame and meaningless through over-use
Colloquial	Everyday, ordinary speech and language
Connotation	Implication or association attached to a word or phrase
Couplet	Two consecutive lines of verse that rhyme

Diction	Type of words, selection of vocabulary, used in a poem
Didactic	A work intended to 'preach', and persuade us towards, a particular moral or political doctrine
Elegy	Serious, meditative poem, usually concerned with the the theme of death
Empathy	A feeling, on the part of the reader, of direct participation in the experience being described. The ability to share the experiences of the poem.
Enjambement	A line of verse that flows uninterruptedly into the following line. Also known as 'run-on' lines
Euphony	Use of pleasant or melodious sounds
Figurative language	Language that departs from the literal, 'dictionary' meaning of the words used
Foot	Basic unit of 'metre'
Hyperbole	Deliberate, extravagant exaggeration
Invective	Use of direct insult, intended to ridicule, denounce or condemn
Invocation	An appeal to a 'higher force' (god, muse, abstraction) to assist the poet's work
Irony	When one thing is stated, yet another meaning — possibly the opposite — is implied
Metaphor	When a word which normally means one thing is made to stand for something else. Because the word retains the sense of its original meaning, it becomes an implied comparison between the associations of the two meanings
Narrative	A piece that tells a story
Onomatopoeia	The use of words whose sounds resemble, or 'act out', their meaning
Oxymoron	Combination of two terms normally considered opposite or incompatible i.e. 'precious dirt', 'delicious sorrow'
Paradox	A statement which appears, at first glance, ridiculous or self-contradictory, yet which, on examination, reveals an unexpected, valid meaning
Pathos	Depth of feeling or emotion; intended to evoke sorrow or pity in the reader
Personification	Attributing feelings, emotions, or sensations to an inanimate object as though it were a living thing

Pun	A play on words that have similar sounds but different meanings
Refrain	Repetition throughout a poem of a phrase, or line, or series of lines, rather like the 'chorus' of a song
Rhetorical Question	One that expects no answer, because the answer is obvious, or implied in the question itself
Simile	A direct comparison between two things, using 'like', or 'as'
Stanza	A division or unit of poem
Stress	This indicates where the rhythmic emphasis is most heavily pronounced in a word
Style	The basic manner in which the poem presents its theme
Subjective	A piece in which the poet presents his own personal thoughts and emotions, his own individual response to what he is describing. If the poet attempts a neutral, detached and comprehensive approach, it may be termed 'Objective'
Symbol	A physical representation of an abstract idea or concept — i.e. the 'rose' for love. Basically, anything that becomes strongly associated with something else in order to illustrate essential qualities or characteristics
Sympathy	Ability to share the feelings of another person
Tone	Poet's attitude to his subject and also the reader
Verse	Poetry in general, not to be used instead of 'stanza'

ACKNOWLEDGEMENTS

We wish to thank the following for permission to reproduce the poems in this book.

Macmillan & Co Ltd, for "The Voice" & "Shadow on the Stone" by Thomas Hardy; Doubleday & Co Inc, for "Mad Song" & "The Tyger" by William Blake; Collins Publishers, for "Devil's Advice to Storytellers" by Robert Graves; Faber & Faber Ltd & Myfanwy Thomas, for "A Gentleman" from *Collected Poems by Edward Thomas*; J.M. Dent, for "Do Not go Gentle into that Good Night" from *Collected Poems by Dylan Thomas*; Reprinted by permission of Faber & Faber Ltd, for "Journey of the Magi" from *Collected Poems 1909-1962 by T.S. Eliot*; for "Musée des Beaux Arts" and "Funeral Blues" from *Collected Poems by W.H. Auden*; for "Follower" from *Death of a Naturalist* by Seamus Heaney; for "He Was" from *Poems 1943-1956* by Richard Wilbur; for "Relic" from *Lupercal* by Ted Hughes; A.P. Watt Ltd & Michael & Anne Yeats, for "When You are Old", "An Irish Airman Foresees His Death" and "Death" from *The Collected Poems of W.B. Yeats*; Reprinted by permission of Oxford University Press, for "Last Mystery" from *Out of Bounds* by Jon Stallworthy, © Oxford University Press 1963; Reprinted by permission of Harvard University Press & the Trustees of Amherst College from *The Poems of Emily Dickinson* edited by Thomas H. Johnson, Cambridge, Mass.: The Belknap Press of Harvard University Press, Copyright 1951, 1955, 1979 by the President & Fellows of Harvard College; Jonathan Cape Ltd & the Executors of the W.H. Davies Estate, for "A Blind Child" from *The Complete Poems of W.H. Davies*; Laurence Pollinger Ltd & the Estate of Frieda Lawrence Ravagli, for "Self-Pity", "Piano" & "Verse 4, Section VII of The Ship of Death" from *The Complete Poems of D.H. Lawrence*; Edinburgh University Press, for "Strawberries" from *The Second Life* by Edwin Morgan; Reprinted by permission of New Directions Publishing Corporation, for "The Loving Dexterity" & "A Negro Woman" by William Carlos Williams, from 'Pictures from Brueghel & Other Poems' Copyright © 1955, 1962 by William Carlos Williams; Lothian Publishing Co Pty Ltd, for "Love's Coming" by John Shaw Neilson; C B Christesen & *Meanjin Quarterly*, University of Melbourne, for "Sea Memory" and The University of Cambridge Local Examinations Syndicate for the past examination questions in Literature.

While every effort has been made to contact the copyright holders of some reproductions, we have been unsuccessful in some instances. To these, we offer our sincere apologies and hope they will take our liberty in good faith.